Pâtisserie OF FRANCE

HILARY WALDEN

McGRAW-HILL BOOK COMPANY

New York   St. Louis   San Francisco
Hamburg   Mexico

All eggs are large unless otherwise stated

First U.S. publication by McGraw-Hill Book Company in 1989

© Macdonald & Co (Publishers) Ltd 1988

First published in Great Britain in 1988
by Macdonald & Co (Publishers) Ltd
London & Sydney

A member of Maxwell Pergamon Publishing Corporation plc

1 2 3 4 5 6 7 8   8 9 2 1 0 9

Library of Congress Cataloging-in-Publication Data

Walden, Hilary.
Pâtisserie of France.
Includes index.
1. Pastry–France   2. Desserts–France.
I. Title
TX773.W285   1989   641.8'65'0944   88-12931

ISBN 0-07-067795-6

Typeset by Tradespools, Frome

Printed and bound in Great Britain by
Purnell Book Production Limited
A member of BPCC plc

Editor: Gillian Prince
Text Editor: Norma MacMillan
Art Director: Bobbie Colegate-Stone
Designer: Frances de Rees
Photographer: Laurie Evans
Stylist: Lesley Richardson
Home Economist: Janice Murfitt

Contents

Introduction

$\sim\!\!\infty\!\!\sim$

France is the home of the classical pâtisserie of haute cuisine, but it also has a centuries-old wealth of traditional cakes, pastries and breads as well as regional specialties. In France, even small villages have at least one pâtissier (often more), who will proudly exhibit his skills in neat displays of meltingly crisp *tartes* filled with sun-ripened fruit, luscious, meticulously decorated gâteaux, butter-rich *sablés*, rum-soaked savarins or other local specialty. If it is someone's wedding day, a Croquembouche may stand supreme in the center of the display.

French housewives are happy to leave the preparation and cooking of pâtisserie to the specialist, and don't mind paying what, in many Americans' opinion, would be high prices. Recipes vary from pâtissier to pâtissier, and each housewife has a favorite on whom she can rely, taking as much pride in his pâtisserie as in her own dishes.

In the mid-seventeenth century, the deep-rooted tradition of baking in France took great strides toward the art of pâtisserie with the publication of two books, *Le Cuisinier François* and *Le Pâtissier François*, both attributed to Pierre La Varenne. These books detailed basic recipes for types of short, puff, choux and raised pie pastry made with oil, two enriched yeast doughs, crèmes pâtissière and frangipane, macaroons and meringues as well as the egg batters which were the forerunners of sponge cakes.

During the eighteenth century, pâtisserie evolved in line with the general mood of the times, with ostentation and show being of prime importance. As elegant tables came into vogue, the dishes that were displayed on them had to be kept in a similar vein – if a dish was to make an impact on tables laden with food, it had to be large and ornate.

Then, in the nineteenth century, under the influence of Marie-Antoine Carême, pâtisserie really developed into a refined skill and art. After the flamboyance of the pre-Revolutionary era and the chaos of the Revolutionary days, the prevailing mood was of more restraint and order. Moreover, the money for, and desirability of, lavish entertaining was diminished.

Following this trend, Carême established discipline in the kitchen and in cooking. He believed the pâtissier should study classical engravings and architecture so that *pièces montées*, the enormous, elaborate replicas of pavilions, bridges and temples, could be constructed with precision after having been drawn to scale first. He both elaborated upon and perfected existing cake and pastry recipes as well as creating some of his own masterpieces, many of which, such as Croquembouche (page 60) and Mille Feuille (page 38), are still popular today.

Carême was not alone in establishing a good reputation for pâtissiers. The decline in the numbers of pâtissiers who could find private employment led more and more of them to open their own establishments, often in close proximity to each other and frequently on the same street, such as the rue St Honoré. Pâtisseries became fashionable and pâtissiers vied with each other in the practice of their art and the creation of new cakes. Savarin and Gâteau St Honoré are just two of the cakes that were developed as specialties at this time.

The refining process was carried further and brought into the twentieth century by that other great chef, Auguste Escoffier, "king of chefs, chef of kings." More modifications have, of course, taken place during the course of this century, but the classical pâtisserie described by Escoffier in his books, particularly the *Guide Culinaire* – which is still considered the "bible" of chefs – is today made as it was then, and is as popular as ever.

I am not a master pâtissière, but I do enjoy good cakes and pastries and I have written this book for people like me. I have based my choice of recipes on the type of pâtisserie that you would expect to find in local bakeries in France – which, I think, are the source of much of the best in pâtisserie.

INGREDIENTS

Butter: As so much butter is used in making pâtisserie, it is important that it be good quality, fresh unsalted butter. French butter is produced from ripened cream, which adds a slight tang to the flavor, whereas sweet cream butters are more commonly used in the United States.

Flour: All-purpose flour is most suitable for pâtes brisée, sucrée and frollée, as well as choux and puff pastries, and cookie recipes; cake flour is best for cake recipes; and strong bread flour should be used for the yeast recipes. Because flours vary in the amount of liquid they will absorb, quantities of liquid, including egg yolk, in a recipe are only a guide: you may find it necessary to add a little less or more.

The inclusion of a small proportion of *potato flour* changes the character of a cake in two ways – it adds lightness and dryness to the texture and a delicate yet discernible sweet nutty note to the flavor. If potato flour is not available, cornstarch can be substituted. Although it has a similar effect on the texture, it has virtually no flavor.

Crème fraîche: Crème fraîche is the type of cream used in France. It has a minimum fat content of 35%, compared with 20.6% in American light coffee or table cream, 31.3% in whipping cream, and 37.6% in heavy cream. Crème fraîche is nearly as thick as heavy cream, but it has a lighter consistency with a slight freshness in flavor that becomes more pronounced as the cream ages.

When using crème fraîche, first stir it to mix in any liquid that is on the surface. When whipping, it may be necessary to add a little milk to soften it (crème fraîche thickens during storage), and care must be taken to avoid it becoming grainy.

Crème fraîche bearing both French and American brand names is becoming more widely available in this country, but if you are unable to find it, a substitute can be made: gently heat heavy cream with half its amount of buttermilk or dairy sour cream, stirring with a wooden spoon, until barely lukewarm (75–85°F). Pour the mixture into a thoroughly cleansed container, partially cover and keep it at the same temperature for 6–8 hours or until the cream has thickened and developed a slightly sharp, but not acidic, flavor. Stir the cream, and keep it in a covered container in the refrigerator for up to 7–10 days. The longer it is kept, the thicker it will become and the sharper the flavor. Some of one batch of crème fraîche can be used to make another.

Fromage blanc/frais: Fromage blanc is really an unflavored type of fromage frais (fresh cheese), but commercially the two names are used interchangeably for plain fresh cheese. The fat content can range from almost nothing (0% *matière grasse*) to 8% (40% *matière grasse*). The latter is the one to use in recipes that are cooked; any can be used in uncooked recipes. Higher fat cream cheese can be substituted.

Sugar: Generally, granulated sugar is used, but superfine is sometimes called for because its fine crystals dissolve easily, not only when heated but also when beaten with egg whites. Vanilla sugar adds a subtle softness to the flavor and couldn't be easier to make – simply pop a vanilla bean in the sugar and keep it in an airtight container for about 5 days before using it. When the sugar has been used, add some more – the bean should remain effective for up to a year.

Nuts: Nuts have a high oil content and become stale and rancid quickly, especially once they have been removed from their shells and with even greater rapidity after they have been ground. So, for the best flavored pâtisserie, when ground nuts are required in a recipe, use freshly skinned (blanched), freshly ground nuts. Take care when handling and grinding nuts, because their high fat content causes them to become oily easily. Grind them in small amounts, as quickly as possible. Normally, I use an old-fashioned hand rotary cheese grater as I find it gives the best results, but if the nuts are to be mixed with flour or sugar, I sometimes mix the flour or sugar with the unground nuts and then grind small amounts in a blender or food processor.

Chocolate: Use the best quality semisweet or bittersweet chocolate that you can find because it will have the fine, bitter flavor that is necessary for good pâtisserie. Do not substitute unsweetened chocolate in these recipes.

Candied, crystallized and glacé peel and fruits: If you do not prepare your own candied, crystallized and glacé peel and fruits, do buy the best that you can find – mass-produced brands found in supermarkets are just not "right" for good French pâtisserie. As well as the more obvious high-class and gourmet food shops, healthfood and wholefood shops often sell well-flavored and succulent peels and fruits.

Praline: To make praline, equal quantities of sugar and nuts, usually almonds although hazelnuts (filberts) or a mixture of nuts may also be used, are heated gently in a heavy-bottomed saucepan while stirring until the sugar melts and then caramelizes to a rich brown and the nuts begin to pop. The mixture is then poured immediately onto a well-oiled marble slab or baking sheet and left to cool and harden. It is then broken up. If a powder is required, for example if it is to be added to a mixture that is to be piped, the praline is ground finely and then sieved. Praline can be prepared in advance and kept in an airtight container.

Almond paste: Simple, uncooked almond paste is easy to make by mixing freshly ground almonds and confectioners' sugar with a little lemon juice and sufficient egg yolk to give a stiff paste. This must not be overmixed, otherwise it will turn oily. A basic recipe is 1½ cups freshly ground almonds, 1 cup confectioners' sugar, a small squeeze of lemon juice and 1 egg yolk. If all of the batch is not required at once, and you are not tempted to make some petits fours with the remainder, it will keep for several days in the refrigerator if well-wrapped in plastic wrap or foil. It then has many uses, for example as a filling for baked apples or apricots.

Apricot glaze: I find it useful to keep some prepared apricot glaze in an airtight non-metallic container so that I always have some handy whenever I need it. For about 1 cup of glaze, gently heat 1 cup of good quality apricot jam in a small, non-aluminum saucepan with about 1½ tbsp of lemon juice and sufficient water or white wine, or a mixture of water or wine with Cognac or an apricot or orange liqueur or Kirsch, to make a thick pourable glaze when melted. Press the jam through a fine non-metallic strainer and store in an airtight container. Warm the glaze gently when needed.

EQUIPMENT

Brioche molds: These are needed to give the characteristic shape of a brioche. The bottom is flat, the sides fluted and flared outwards, which also gives the dough plenty of room to spread out as it rises. Brioche molds come in various sizes from individual ones, about 2¼ inches across the top, upwards.

Kugelhopf pans: These decorative pans have flutes that swirl around the sides and a funnel in the center which conducts the heat to the center of the mixture being baked ensuring that it cooks evenly.

Large metal spoon: A large metal spoon of the type that chefs use is invaluable for efficiently, yet delicately, lifting, folding and blending light mixtures, such as meringues or sponges, of more than about 2-egg quantities.

Ovens: Very few ovens have accurate thermostats – mine doesn't, I know. Most people become accustomed to the everyday peculiarities of their ovens and make the adjustments to cooking temperatures and times given in recipes. This practice is all right for dishes

Rum Babas

Large & Small Brioches

such as casseroles, but with some sensitive pâtisserie it can result in failure and disappointment. So I would advise you to invest in an oven thermometer. However, even this does not do away with the need to keep an eye on the baking because of the difficulty of being precise about timings.

BAKING HINTS

Pastries

When making puff pastry, pâte brisée, pâte sucrée and pâte frollée, coolness of ingredients, equipment and atmosphere and quick, light, sensitive handling are of paramount importance. Should the pastry become at all sticky, cover it immediately and place it in the refrigerator to firm up. The pastry should also be placed, covered, in the refrigerator before it is rolled out for the final shaping and again afterward, before it is baked.

Puff pastry must also be chilled in between the rollings and foldings. If the pastry is left so long in the refrigerator that it becomes hard, allow it to soften a little at room temperature before rolling it out. Pâtes brisée, sucrée and frollée are fragile when they are taken from the oven so leave them to stand for a few minutes before moving them.

To prevent pastry from becoming soggy when filled with a cooked or liquid filling, such as a custard mixture, bake it "blind" first (see page 13). Once a filling has been added, the pastry must be baked immediately. Further insurance against soggy pastry is given by brushing the baked pastry with egg white and never putting a hot filling in a pastry case, whether raw or baked.

Pastries are at their best if eaten fresh from the oven, either while still warm or within a few hours. Choux pastries should be eaten within an hour or so of filling; the same applies to puff pastries that are filled after baking, such as Mille Feuille (page 38).

To Line a Flan Ring or Tart Pan

Butter the flan ring, then place it on a buttered baking sheet, or butter a tart pan that has a removable base.

On a lightly floured surface, using a lightly floured rolling pin, roll out the dough thinly to about 1½–2 inches larger than the diameter of the ring or pan. Lightly brush away any surplus flour from the surface of the dough.

Carefully roll the dough back over the rolling pin and lift it over the center of the ring or pan. Unroll the dough from the rolling pin and allow it to fall loosely to the shape of the ring. Working from the center, carefully ease the dough into shape, gently but firmly pressing it into the angle between the base and the sides so that it fits snugly. If using a fluted flan ring or tart pan, pay particular attention to easing the dough into the curves, especially at the bottom. Leave the dough to relax for 20 minutes or so, then remove the excess dough by passing the rolling pin quickly and firmly across the top of the flan ring or pan. Lightly prick the bottom with the tines of a fork, cover and chill.

N.B. The thickness of the pastry will vary according not only to the type of pastry but also to the particular use to which it is being put – different tarts are more enjoyable with different thicknesses of pastry.

To Line Tartlet or Barquette Molds

Group the molds together on a baking sheet. Roll out the pastry thinly, fold it back over the rolling pin and lift it over the molds, then unroll it on to them. With a small ball of floured dough, ease the pastry into the shape of the molds. Roll the rolling pin firmly over the top of the molds to remove excess pastry.

To Bake Blind

Lay a piece of parchment paper on the bottom of the pastry case and cover with just enough pie weights or dried beans to weight the pastry down. (Pastry in tartlet and barquette molds need only be pricked with the tines of a fork.) To *part-bake:* Bake in a preheated oven for about 10 minutes or until the pastry is set and very lightly colored. Remove the weights or beans and paper. If the pastry in the bottom of the case appears to be too pale, return it to the oven for a few minutes to color a little more.

If the pastry case is to be completely baked blind, return it to the oven to bake for a further 10–15 minutes after removing the lining paper, until it is a light golden brown and completely set. Tartlet and barquette cases will take 10–15 minutes baking in all.

Meringues

The temperature of the ingredients is not vital to the success of meringue, but if the egg whites are at room temperature rather than at refrigerator temperature they will be easier to beat to a foam. The proportion of sugar that is added determines the final texture of the meringue – 2 tbsp per egg white produces a soft meringue, 4 tbsp a hard one. Sugar helps to protect the meringue from drainage and collapse, but it also reduces the foaming of the egg whites so it should not be added until the final stages of the beating.

The addition of a small amount of acid, such as a pinch of cream of tartar or a few drops of lemon juice or a mild vinegar, helps to guard against overbeating and the overcoagulation of the egg whites that results in lumpiness, collapse of the meringue and seeping of liquid.

Fat retards the beating of the whites, so be sure bowl and whisk are scrupulously clean. Although salt enhances the flavor of foods, it should not be added to meringues as it decreases their stability.

Sweet Pie Pastry

Pastry Slice with Summer Fruits

TRANCHE DES FRUITS D'ETE

A rectangular version of a tart ring is used here, and it must be buttered and placed on a baking sheet before it is lined with pastry. A rectangular tart pan with a removable base, often called a tranche mold, may also be used.

SERVES 8

1 quantity Pâte Frollée (page 121)	whipped cream, broken macaroons and fine chocolate caraque, to decorate (optional)
⅔ cup crème fraîche or heavy cream	
1 quantity warm Crème Frangipane, made with macaroons (page 117)	
	Glaze
1 tbsp butter	6 tbsp currant jelly
about 3 cups summer fruits, e.g. strawberries, raspberries, loganberries, boysenberries, etc.	small squeeze of lemon juice

Roll out the pastry on a lightly floured surface, using a lightly floured rolling pin, and line a buttered 14 × 4½ inch rectangular flan form placed on a baking sheet, or a tranche mold. Prick the bottom with the tines of a fork. Cover and chill for 30 minutes.

Preheat the oven to 400°F.

Bake the pastry case blind for 20–25 minutes until lightly colored. Allow to cool slightly, then carefully transfer to a wire rack to cool completely.

Whip the crème fraîche or cream until it just forms peaks, then whisk into the crème frangipane until smooth. Dot the butter over the surface and leave to cool completely.

For the glaze, gently warm the currant jelly with a small squeeze of lemon juice. Brush about 2 tbsp of glaze over the inside of the pastry case. Leave until it is quite cold, and allow the remaining glaze to cool slightly.

Whisk the butter into the frangipane mixture, then spread the mixture over the bottom of the pastry case. Smooth the surface, then arrange the fruit neatly in rows on top. Brush the fruit with the remaining glaze.

Decorate the tranche with whipped cream, piped through a star tube, broken macaroons and fine chocolate caraque, if liked.

Pastry Slice with Summer Fruits

$\mathcal{A}$pricot Tart

── TARTE AUX ABRICOTS ──

T his tart is equally delicious served warm or cold, but must be eaten on the day of making. If the apricots are a little lacking in flavor, add 2 or 3 tbsp of apricot brandy to the wine while the apricots are cooling. If you have a sweet tooth and the apricots are a little sharp, dissolve 3–4 tablespoons sugar in the wine before poaching the fruit.

SERVES 6–8

Pâte sucrée	Filling
1¼ cups all-purpose flour	1¼ lb ripe apricots
pinch of salt	2½ cups good dessert wine
6 tbsp unsalted butter	1 vanilla bean
3 small egg yolks	1¼ cups crème fraîche or
¼ cup vanilla sugar	heavy cream
1 egg white, lightly beaten	4 tbsp unsalted butter, melted
	3 egg yolks
	about 3–4 tbsp vanilla sugar
	6 tbsp Apricot Glaze made with
	white wine (page 9), warmed

Make the pastry with the flour, salt, butter, egg yolks and sugar, according to the instructions on page 121. Cover and chill for 30 minutes.

Score the apricots around the groove, twist them in half and remove the pits. In a skillet, gently heat the wine with the vanilla bean to just below simmering point. Lower the apricot halves into the wine syrup and poach gently for 5–8 minutes, depending on the ripeness of the fruit. Leave to cool in the wine, then using a slotted spoon transfer to a wire rack placed over a tray and leave to drain.

Butter a 10 inch flan ring placed on a baking sheet, or tart pan with a removable base. Use the pastry to line the flan ring or pan. Chill for 30 minutes.

Preheat the oven to 400°F. Part-bake the pastry case blind for 10 minutes. Brush the pastry case with lightly beaten egg white. Reduce the oven temperature to 350°F.

Stir the crème fraîche or cream and melted butter together, then stir into the egg yolks and add vanilla sugar to taste. Arrange the apricots in the pastry case, pour the custard over and bake for about 35 minutes or until the filling is lightly set.

Leave to stand for a few minutes, then brush lightly with warm apricot glaze before transferring to a wire rack to cool.

Rhubarb Cream Tart

—————— TARTE ALSACIENNE ——————

Although rhubarb is not generally used much in French cooking in general, it is very popular in Alsace and Lorraine, particularly to flavor a creamy-custard tart where its acidity provides a contrast to the sweet crispness of the pastry and the rich smoothness of the custard. The problem of excess wateriness that is associated with rhubarb is solved by sprinkling it with sugar about 30 minutes before using.

SERVES 6–8

Pâte brisée	*Filling*
1¼ cups all-purpose flour	⅔ cup sugar
small pinch of salt	1½ lb rhubarb, cut into 1 inch
7 tbsp unsalted butter	lengths
2 small egg yolks	3 eggs, separated
1 egg white, lightly beaten	¼ cup crème fraîche or heavy cream

Make the pastry with the flour, salt, butter and egg yolks, according to the instructions on page 120. Cover and chill for 30 minutes.

Butter a 10 inch tart ring placed on a baking sheet, or tart pan with a removable base. Use the pastry to line the flan ring or pan, then cover and chill for 30 minutes.

Preheat the oven to 400°F.

Sprinkle half of the sugar over the rhubarb and leave for 30 minutes.

Meanwhile, part-bake the pastry case blind for 10 minutes. Brush with lightly beaten egg white and leave to cool.

Drain the rhubarb, reserving the juices, and place in a single layer in the pastry case. Sprinkle with half of the remaining sugar and cook in the oven for 15–20 minutes or until the fruit is beginning to soften.

Blend the egg yolks with the remaining sugar, reserved rhubarb juices and the crème fraîche or cream. Beat the egg whites until stiff but not dry, then fold into the cream mixture. Pour over the rhubarb and bake for a further 20–30 minutes or until the filling is just set.

Leave to stand for a few minutes before transferring to a wire rack. Serve warm or cold.

Lemon Tart

———— TARTE AU CITRON ————

If your oven tends to be on the "hot" side, reduce the temperature further when cooking the filling otherwise it may bubble over or color too quickly.

SERVES 6–8

1 quantity Pâte Sucrée, made with	*To decorate*
2 tbsp sugar	2 thin-skinned lemons
1 egg white, lightly beaten	¾ cup sugar
3 eggs	1½ cups water
1 egg yolk	1 lemon, thinly sliced
¾ cup sugar	
finely grated zest and strained juice of 3 lemons and 1 orange	
¾ cup crème fraîche or heavy cream	

For the decoration, pare the zest from one of the lemons very thinly using a potato peeler, making sure that none of the white pith is included. Cut the zest into very fine shreds, then blanch three times, in fresh water each time and rinsing well after each blanching. Drain.

Gently heat ⅓ cup of the sugar in ½ cup of the water, stirring with a wooden spoon until the sugar has dissolved, then bring to a boil and boil, without stirring, for 1 minute. Add the lemon zest shreds and simmer very gently until they are tender and translucent. Remove from the syrup. Drain on a wire rack.

Meanwhile, peel both of the lemons, making sure that all the pith has been removed, then divide into segments. Gently heat the remaining sugar in the remaining water, stirring with a wooden spoon until the sugar has dissolved, then bring to a boil without stirring. Reduce the heat so the syrup barely simmers, then lower in the lemon segments using a slotted spoon and cook gently for about 3–4 minutes. Lift from the syrup and leave to drain on a wire rack placed over a tray.

Butter a deep 8 inch tart pan. Use the pastry to line the pan, then cover and chill for 30 minutes.

Preheat the oven to 400°F. Part-bake the pastry case blind for 10 minutes. Brush the bottom of the pastry case with beaten egg white, then leave to cool to room temperature. Reduce the oven temperature to 300°F.

Blend the eggs and egg yolk with the sugar until it has dissolved, then beat in the fruit zest and juices and the crème fraîche or cream. With the tart shell still in its pan, placed on a baking sheet, pour in most of the filling. Carefully place the baking sheet on an oven shelf and spoon in the remaining filling. Slide the oven shelf into position and bake for 25–30 minutes or until the filling is just set (test it by shaking it gently).

Leave to stand for several minutes before transferring to a wire rack to cool.

Decorate the tart with the lemon segments and slices and shreds of zest.

Caramelized Strawberry Tart

———————— TARTE AUX FRAISES CARAMELISEE ————————

Other fruits can be used instead of strawberries, such as an equal weight of raspberries or about eight peeled and sliced peaches. As it is vital that the custard does not boil, you may find it easier to cook it in a bowl placed over a saucepan of hot, not boiling, water or in a double boiler or bain-marie.

SERVES 6–8

1 quantity Pâte Frollée (page 121)
1 egg white, lightly beaten
1¼ cups heavy cream
1 vanilla bean, split
3 egg yolks
about 3 tbsp sugar
2 heaping cups strawberries
extra sugar, to sprinkle

Butter a 9 inch tart ring placed on a baking sheet, or tart pan with a removable base. Use the pastry to line the flan ring or pan and prick the bottom with the tines of a fork. Cover and chill for 30 minutes.

Preheat the oven to 400°F.

Bake the pastry case blind for 20–25 minutes. Brush it lightly with beaten egg white and leave to stand for a few minutes, then transfer to a wire rack to cool completely.

Gently heat the cream with the vanilla bean to simmering point in a heavy-bottomed saucepan. Remove from the heat, cover and leave to infuse for 20 minutes. Remove the vanilla bean.

Beat the egg yolks and sugar until very thick and light. Heat the cream to just below boiling point, then slowly pour onto the egg yolks, stirring continuously. Pour back into the rinsed pan and cook very gently, stirring, until the custard coats the back of the spoon. On no account allow the custard to boil. Pass through a strainer, cover the surface closely with plastic wrap and leave to cool.

Halve, quarter or slice the strawberries, then lay most of them in the bottom of the tart case. Pour the custard over the fruit, smooth the top and chill well.

Just before serving, sprinkle a thick layer of sugar over the top and place close to a very hot broiler for 1–2 minutes or until the sugar caramelizes. Decorate with the remaining strawberries.

Apple Tart

TARTE AUX POMMES

It is important to get the correct acidity/sweetness balance between the pastry, apple purée, sliced apples and glaze (neither the apple purée nor the sliced apples should be too sweet), so taste where appropriate.

SERVES 6

1 quantity Pâte Sucrée, made with 2 tbsp sugar (page 121)	*Sliced apple*
	1¼ lb well-flavored, crisp, tart
1 egg white, lightly beaten	apples
6 tbsp Apricot Glaze (page 9), warmed	4 tbsp unsalted butter, melted
	2 tbsp sugar
Apple purée	
1½ lb baking apples	
about 2 tbsp sugar	

Butter an 8 inch tart pan with a removable base. Use the pastry to line the pan. Cover and chill for 30 minutes.

Preheat the oven to 400°F.

For the apple purée, peel the apples, remove the cores and chop the flesh. Cook gently with 1 tbsp water in a wide pan for about 10 minutes, stirring with a fork occasionally toward the end of the cooking to break up the pieces and prevent sticking. Remove from the heat when some of the apple is just partially broken. Add sugar to taste, remembering that the purée should not be too sweet and beat with a spoon until smooth. Pour into a bowl and leave until cold.

Part-bake the pastry case blind for 10 minutes. Brush the pastry with lightly beaten egg white, then leave to cool. Lower the oven temperature to 375°F.

Spoon the apple purée into the pastry case.

Peel the tart apples, cut into halves and remove the cores, then cut into approximately ⅙–¼ inch slices. Arrange the slices on the apple purée, starting at the outside edge, in concentric circles, overlapping the slices and the circles. Brush lightly with melted butter, sprinkle the sugar over and bake for 25–35 minutes or until the apple slices are just becoming tender.

Leave the tart to stand for a few minutes before removing the side of the pan and carefully slipping the tart onto a wire rack to cool.

Just before serving, brush warm apricot glaze lightly but evenly over the surface.

Normandy Apple Tart

—————— TARTE AUX POMMES NORMANDE ——————

*D*ishes that include apples feature very strongly in the traditional cooking of Normandy, the apple growing region of France. Although this recipe is from the area, I don't doubt that you will find many different versions of Normandy Apple Tart.

SERVES 6–8

1 quantity Pâte Sucrée, made with	*Filling*
1 tbsp vanilla sugar	7 tbsp unsalted butter,
(page 121)	at room temperature
1 egg white, lightly beaten	7 tbsp sugar
4 ripe apples	3 egg yolks, beaten
sugar, to sprinkle	2 tbsp Calvados
6 tbsp Apricot Glaze (page 9),	2 tbsp crème fraîche or heavy cream
warmed	1–1⅓ cups freshly ground almonds

Use the pastry to line a buttered 9 inch flan ring placed on a baking sheet, or tart pan with a removable base. Cover and chill for 30 minutes.

Preheat the oven to 400°F.

For the filling, beat the butter until softened, then add the sugar and beat until fluffy and light. Gradually add the egg yolks, beating well after each addition. Add the Calvados and crème fraîche or cream, then gently fold in the ground almonds. Brush the bottom of the pastry case with egg white, then spoon in the filling and level the surface.

Peel, halve and core the apples, then cut them into very thin slices, keeping the halves together. Still keeping each half of apple together, place one half on the filling in the center and arrange the other halves radiating from the center like the spokes of a wheel. Press the slices down lightly into the filling.

Bake for 12–15 minutes, then lower the heat to 350°F. Sprinkle sugar over the apples and continue baking until the filling is set, the apples are tender and the top is lightly caramelized, about 15 minutes.

Transfer the tart to a wire rack. Just before serving, brush the top lightly with apricot glaze.

Peach and Almond Custard Tart

——————— TARTE AUX PECHES BOURDALOUE ———————

*T*he rue Bourdaloue was one of the streets in Paris famed for its pâtisseries during the nineteenth century, but the name "Bourdaloue" was applied to pâtisseries before that date and probably originated with a seventeenth-century preacher. Apricots and pears can be prepared in the same way.

SERVES 4–6

1 quantity Pâte Sucrée, made with 2 tbsp sugar (page 121)
½ cup vanilla sugar
1 quart water
4–6 ripe peaches, depending on size
4 tbsp Cognac
1 egg white, lightly beaten
1 quantity Crème Frangipane, made with 2 oz or about 3 macaroons (page 117)
½ cup sliced almonds
confectioners' sugar, to dredge

Butter a 9 inch tart ring placed on a baking sheet, or a tart pan with a removable base. Use the pastry to line the tart ring or pan, cover and chill for 30 minutes.

Preheat the oven to 400°F.

Gently heat the vanilla sugar and water in a deep wide skillet or a large saucepan, stirring with a wooden spoon until it dissolves. Bring to a boil without stirring, then leave to simmer for about 5 minutes while preparing the peaches. Cut the peaches around the groove, twist them in half and remove the pits. Reduce the heat beneath the syrup, lower in the peaches and poach gently for 5–10 minutes or until just tender. Remove the peaches using a slotted spoon and allowing excess syrup to drain off, then peel them and cut into slices. Lay the slices in a shallow bowl. Sprinkle the Cognac over and leave to cool.

Bake the pastry case blind for 20–25 minutes. Brush egg white lightly over the pastry case, transfer to a wire rack and leave to cool.

Lift the peaches from the bowl using a slotted spoon, allowing excess liquid to drain off, and place them on paper towels to drain. Stir the liquid into the crème frangipane.

Pour a layer of crème frangipane into the pastry case. Arrange the peaches, overlapping if necessary, over the entire surface, then cover with the remaining crème. Scatter the almonds over the top and sift confectioners' sugar over so that some of the almonds show through. Place under a hot broiler to glaze the top and toast the exposed almonds.

Illustrated on page 26

Walnut and Pear Tart

LE POIRAT

*T*his tart can also be called picquenchagne (which may also be spelled picanchagne), depending on whether it is made in the Bourbonnais or in Berry. To complicate matters further, again depending on where it is made, Le Poirat may contain apples or quinces or may be based on a yeast pastry. Use a rounded variety of pear, such as Comice, rather than a longer, thinner type such as Bosc.

SERVES 6

Pastry	Filling
1⅔ cups all-purpose flour	1½ lb pears
pinch of salt	2 tbsp eau-de-vie de poire William or
1 stick unsalted butter, diced	Cognac
2 egg yolks, lightly beaten	1 tbsp vanilla sugar
⅔ cup finely ground walnuts	freshly ground black pepper
6 tbsp vanilla sugar	⅔ cup crème fraîche or heavy cream
1 egg white, lightly beaten	
extra sugar, to sprinkle	

Make the pastry with the flour, salt, butter, egg yolks, walnuts and sugar as for Pâte Frollée on page 121.

Peel the pears, cut into quarters and remove the cores. Sprinkle the eau-de-vie or Cognac over and leave for 1 hour.

Butter a 9 inch tart ring placed on a baking sheet, or a tart pan with a removable base. Use about two-thirds of the pastry to line the tart ring or pan. Roll out the rest of the pastry to form a lid. Using a 1 inch cutter, remove a circle from the center. Cover and chill the lined pan and the lid for 30 minutes.

Preheat the oven to 375°F.

Lift the pears from the eau-de-vie or Cognac using a slotted spoon (reserve the liquid) and arrange them like the spokes of a wheel in the pastry case, including some pear as the hub of the wheel. Sprinkle the sugar over the pears, then grind a fine sprinkling of black pepper over them.

Dampen the edges of the pastry case and place the lid centrally over the pie. Press the edges together to seal them firmly. Decorate with pastry trimmings, if liked. Bake for 20–25 minutes or until the pastry is beginning to brown. Brush lightly with beaten egg white, sprinkle with sugar and return to the oven to bake for about 10 minutes longer or until the pastry is browned and crisp and the pears tender.

Whip the crème fraîche or heavy cream lightly with the reserved eau-de-vie or Cognac.

Leave the tart to stand for a few minutes before removing it from the pan, then serve warm with the cream mixture poured through the hole in the lid.

Illustrated on page 27

Peach and Almond Custard Tart

Walnut and Pear Tart

Fresh Cheese Tart

———————— TARTE AU FROMAGE BLANC ————————

*T*o *drain the cheese, spoon it into a non-metallic sieve lined with cheesecloth, place over a bowl, and leave, covered, in a cool place, but not the refrigerator, for a few hours.*

SERVES 6

Pâte brisée	Filling
¾ cup all-purpose flour	2 oz (about ½ cup) wild strawberries
small pinch of salt	2 eggs, separated
5 tbsp unsalted butter, diced	½ cup granulated sugar
1 small egg yolk	½ lb drained fromage blanc or
	fromage frais, or cream cheese
	¼ cup light cream
	extra granulated sugar, to sprinkle
	⅓ cup slivered almonds
	confectioners' sugar, to dredge
	wild strawberries, to decorate

Butter an 8 inch tart ring placed on a baking sheet, or a tart pan with a removable base.

Make the pastry with the flour, salt, butter and egg yolk, according to the instructions on page 120. Cover and chill for 30 minutes, then use to line the flan ring or pan. Prick the bottom with the tines of a fork, then cover and chill again for 30 minutes.

Preheat the oven to 350°F.

For the filling, purée the wild strawberries and pass through a non-metallic sieve. Beat the egg yolks and sugar together, then beat in the cheese with the cream and continue to beat until light and fluffy. Beat the egg whites until they just begin to hold firm peaks, then quickly and lightly fold into the cheese mixture until just evenly blended.

Sprinkle granulated sugar over the bottom of the pastry case, then spread the wild strawberry purée over. Fill with the cheese mixture and bake for 10 minutes. Reduce the oven temperature to 300°F and bake for a further 35–40 minutes or until the center is just set. Leave to cool in the oven, with the heat turned off and the door open.

Just before serving, scatter the almonds over the top, sift confectioners' sugar over and place under a very hot broiler for a minute or so to caramelize the sugar. Decorate the top with extra wild strawberries.

Goat's Cheese Tart

─── TOURTEAU POITOU ───

*F*resh goat's cheese will add a tang to the flavor of this specialty from Poitou without making it *taste at all "goaty." Traditionally, the crust should be almost black – but if the one that you are baking isn't by the time the filling is cooked, place the tourteau under a very hot broiler for a minute or two.*

SERVES 4–5

1 quantity Pâte Brisée (page 120)
5 oz fresh goat's cheese
1 tbsp unsalted butter, just melted
2 eggs
3 tbsp sugar
6 tbsp all-purpose flour
½ tsp baking powder

Butter a deep 6 inch tart ring placed on a baking sheet, or a tart pan with a removable base. Use the pastry to line the tart ring or pan, cover and chill for 30 minutes.

Preheat the oven to 400°F.

Mix the cheese and butter together in a blender until smooth.

Beat the eggs and sugar together until thick and light and the mixture will upsport a trail when the beater is lifted from it. Fold in the cheese mixture until just evenly blended. Sift the flour and baking powder over the surface and lightly fold into the mixture until just evenly blended. Pour into the pastry case and bake for 35–45 minutes or until the filling is set in the center and the crust well colored. If the top is not really dark, place the tourteau under a very hot broiler for 1–2 minutes to give it the traditional appearance.

Leave to stand for a few minutes before transferring to a wire rack to cool. Eat fresh.

Rum Custard Cake

──────── GATEAU BASQUE ────────

*T*he *"hall-mark" of a Gâteau Basque is the lattice pattern that is traditionally traced with the tines of a fork on the crust.*

SERVES 6–8

1 quantity warm Crème Pâtissière (page 116)
1 tsp finely grated lemon zest
2 tbsp dark rum
double quantity Pâte Sucrée, made with ¼ cup sugar (page 121)
1 egg, lightly beaten with 1 tsp cold water, to glaze

Flavor the crème pâtissière with the lemon zest and rum and leave to cool completely.

Preheat the oven to 350°F.

Butter an 8–9 inch round cake pan that is about 2 inches deep, preferably with a loose bottom.

Use about two-thirds of the pastry to line the cake pan, easing the pastry up the sides so that it stands slightly above the height of the pan. Fill the pastry case with the crème pâtissière. Roll out the remaining pastry to a thin round of the same diameter as the pan. Fold it back over the rolling pin, lift it centrally over the pan and lay it over the filling. Press the edges of the lining pastry and the lid firmly together to seal them, to prevent the filling from bubbling through. Brush the top lightly with the egg glaze, then carefully mark a lattice design on the top with the tines of a fork.

Bake for about 45 minutes, covering the top with parchment paper or foil if it browns too soon.

Leave to cool slightly, then carefully remove from the pan and leave, right side uppermost, to cool on a wire rack. Serve at room temperature.

$\mathscr{G}$ascon Prune Tart

———— TARTE AUX PRUNEAUX GASCONNE ————

The particular variety of plum tree that produces pruneaux d'Agen, the prune d'Ente, was first introduced into the Armagnac area during the Middle Ages, but it was not until the sixteenth century when the monks of Clairac, near Tonniens, planted the first orchards, that these plums were cultivated to any great extent. By the eighteenth century they were an established regional specialty, and recipes that include prunes feature prominently in the local cooking.

SERVES 6

4 tbsp Armagnac
2 tbsp hot water
¾ lb pitted Agen prunes
1 quantity Pâte Frollée (page 121)
6 tbsp crème fraîche or whipping cream
2 eggs, beaten
2 tbsp vanilla sugar
2 tbsp unsalted butter, just melted
orange flower water
¾ cup roughly chopped, toasted blanched almonds
whipped cream, to serve

Sprinkle the Armagnac and hot water over the prunes and leave to soak, stirring occasionally.

Butter a 9 inch tart ring placed on a baking sheet, or a tart pan with a removable base. Use the pastry to line the tart ring or pan, cover and chill for 30 minutes.

Preheat the oven to 400°F.

Part-bake the pastry case blind for 10 minutes, then leave to cool. Lower the oven temperature to 325°F.

Remove the prunes from the soaking liquid using a slotted spoon (reserve the liquid), dry on paper towels and place in the pastry case. Whisk together the crème fraîche or cream, reserved liquid, eggs, sugar and butter. Add orange flower water to taste, then fold in the almonds. Pour the filling over the prunes. Bake for about 30 minutes or until the filling is lightly set.

Serve warm, decorated with whipped cream or with the cream served separately.

Raspberry Tartlets

———————— TARTELETTES AUX FRAMBOISES ————————

The addition of beaten egg white lightens the filling. It is traditional to brush the fruit with currant glaze, but if you use really fresh raspberries that are full of flavor, I think this detracts from the true delicious raspberry fruitiness.

MAKES 8–10

1 quantity Pâte Sucrée (page 121)
¼ lb fresh cream cheese such as Petits-Suisses
½ cup crème fraîche or heavy cream
1 egg white
about 1 tbsp vanilla sugar
1 pint raspberries
¼ cup currant jelly, melted (optional)

Use the pastry to line 8–10 buttered tartlet molds that are 3 inches in diameter. Prick the bottoms with a fork, cover and chill for about 30 minutes.

Preheat the oven to 400°F.

Bake the tartlet cases blind for 10–15 minutes or until a light golden brown. Leave to cool for a few minutes, then transfer to a wire rack to cool.

Blend the cheese with the crème fraîche or cream until smooth, then whip lightly with a balloon or flat whisk. Beat the egg white until soft peaks are formed. Sprinkle the sugar over and beat again for about 30 seconds until shiny. Lightly fold into the cheese mixture using a metal spoon, then divide evenly between the tartlet cases.

Arrange the raspberries on top and brush lightly with melted currant jelly, if used.

Illustrated on page 34

Fruit Barquettes

──────── BARQUETTES AUX FRUITS ────────

These attractively shaped tartlets really make the most of soft summer fruits and look beautiful served on a large plate lined with fresh leaves. Decorate them with tiny sprigs of mint – especially good with black currants – instead of whipped cream if you prefer.

MAKES ABOUT 14

1 quantity Pâte Frollée made with hazelnuts (page 121)
⅔ cup heavy cream
1 tbsp vanilla confectioners' sugar
¼ cup currant jelly, melted
about 3 cups prepared fruit such as raspberries, sliced strawberries, wild strawberries, red currants, seedless or seeded grapes, black currants

Butter 14 barquette molds that are 4 inches long. Use the pastry to line the molds. Cover and chill for 30 minutes.

Preheat the oven to 400°F.

Bake the barquette cases blind for 10–15 minutes. Leave to cool for 1–2 minutes, then transfer to a wire rack to cool completely.

Whip the cream until it just begins to thicken, then add the sugar and whip until the cream stands in soft peaks. Spoon into a pastry bag fitted with a small star tube.

Lightly brush the insides of the barquette cases with warmed currant jelly, then fill with the fruit. Decorate with piped cream.

Illustrated on page 35

Raspberry Tartlets

Cherry Tartlets & Fruit Barquettes

$\mathscr{C}$herry Tartlets

-------------------- TARTELETTES AUX CERISES --------------------

T   *he affinity of chocolate and cherries is well known and in this recipe it also provides a delicious contrast to the smooth creamy filling, as well as protecting the pastry against becoming soggy. Pâte Sucrée can be replaced by Pâte Frollée (page 121): reduce the flour to 1 cup and add ⅔ cup ground almonds.*

MAKES 12–14

Pâte sucrée	Filling
1⅓ cups all-purpose flour	about 3 oz semisweet chocolate,
pinch of salt	chopped
7 tbsp unsalted butter	½ lb fromage blanc or frais, or cream
3 egg yolks	cheese
5 tbsp sugar	¼ cup sugar, or to taste
	⅔ cup crème fraîche or heavy cream
	1¼ lb (3½ cups) ripe sweet cherries,
	preferably dark, pitted
	black cherry jelly if dark cherries
	have been used, currant jelly if paler
	cherries have been used, melted
	(optional)

Make the pastry with the flour, salt, butter, egg yolks and sugar according to the instructions on page 121. Cover and chill for 30 minutes.

Butter 12–14 deep 3 inch tartlet molds. Use the pastry to line the tartlet molds, cover and chill for 30 minutes.

Preheat the oven to 400°F.

Bake the tartlet cases blind for 10–15 minutes. Leave to stand for 1–2 minutes, then transfer to a wire rack to cool.

Melt the chocolate in a bowl placed over a saucepan of hot but not boiling water. Using a pastry brush, paint a thin layer of chocolate over the insides of the tartlet cases. Leave to set and harden.

Beat the fromage blanc or frais with the sugar. Whip the crème fraîche or cream until it stands in peaks, then fold into the cheese mixture. Divide between the tartlet cases and arrange the cherries on top. Brush with melted jelly, if liked.

Illustrated on page 35

Caramel Cream and Walnut Pastries

LAVARDINS

These pastries, with their caramelized cream and walnut filling, are sweet and rich, food for adults rather than children. The confectioners' sugar is blended with lemon juice to add a little sharpness, but you could use water if you prefer.

MAKES ABOUT 9

Pâte brisée	Filling
1⅓ cups all-purpose flour	1 cup sugar
pinch of salt	1 tsp lemon juice
1 stick unsalted butter	2 tbsp water
1 egg yolk	1 cup heavy cream
2 tbsp cold water	2 cups chopped walnuts
1 egg, lightly beaten with 1 tsp water, to glaze	3 tbsp butter
	Icing
	about 1 cup confectioners' sugar, sifted
	1–2 tbsp lemon juice

Make the pastry with the flour, salt, butter, egg yolk and water according to the instructions on page 120. Cover and chill for 30 minutes.

To make the filling, gently heat the sugar with the lemon juice and water in a large, heavy-bottomed saucepan, stirring with a wooden spoon until the sugar has dissolved. Bring to a boil without stirring, until the syrup turns to a rich brown caramel. Immediately remove the pan from the heat and pour in the cream – it will bubble and splutter. Swirl the pan until the spluttering stops, then return to the heat and boil, without stirring, until the temperature reaches 240°F. Remove from the heat and stir in the walnuts and butter. Pour into a large bowl and leave to cool completely.

Roll out two-thirds of the dough on a lightly floured surface, using a lightly floured rolling pin, and line about 9 tartlet molds that are 3 inches in diameter. Prick the bottoms lightly with the tines of a fork, cover and chill for 30 minutes. Roll out the remaining pastry and cut out lids for the tartlets. Cover and chill.

Preheat the oven to 400°F.

Bake the tartlet cases blind for 10 minutes. Leave to cool.

Divide the filling between the tartlet cases. Dampen the edges of the pastry, then place the lids in position and press the edges together firmly to seal them well. Bake for about 15 minutes longer or until the tops are lightly browned. Leave the pastries to stand for a few minutes before transferring to a wire rack to cool slightly until warm.

Blend the confectioners' sugar with sufficient lemon juice to make an icing that will coat the back of the spoon. Pour the icing over the lavardins and serve.

Puff Pastry

Puff Pastry Slice with Fruit

――――――――― MILLE FEUILLE AUX FRUITS ―――――――――

You may find it easier and more practical to divide the unbaked dough into three equal pieces and then to roll out each piece to whatever dimensions you choose (the thickness is more important than the actual size or shape); trim the edges and corners as in the method. Pastry rolled to a round is customarily called a Gâteau Mille Feuille. Serve the pastry soon after it has been assembled, and use a large serrated knife to cut it.

SERVES 8–10

1 quantity Puff Pastry (page 123)
⅓ cup heavy cream
1½ cups confectioners' sugar, sifted
1 quantity Crème Pâtissière (page 116)
about 3 cups strawberries or other prepared fresh fruit, such as raspberries, wild strawberries, peaches, cherries etc. or a combination of fruits
a few strawberry leaves and flowers, if available, or mint leaves, to decorate

Roll out the pastry on a lightly floured surface, using a lightly floured rolling pin, to a large rectangle about ⅛ inch thick. Using a sharp knife, trim the edges and corners to make sure they are all square. Carefully transfer the pastry to a dampened baking sheet making sure the shape remains true. Prick the surface all over with the tines of a fork, cover and chill for 30 minutes.

Preheat the oven to 425°F.

Bake the pastry for 10–15 minutes or until crisp and golden brown. Transfer to a wire rack to cool. When cold, use a large, sharp knife to trim the edges and to cut into three equal rectangles. Keep the trimmings.

Whip the cream with 2 tbsp of the confectioners' sugar until soft peaks are formed. Lightly fold into the crème pâtissière.

Place one pastry rectangle on a serving plate and spread half of the cream mixture over. Reserve a few berries for decoration, and slice or cut the remaining berries according to size. Lay half of them on the cream. Cover with another piece of pastry and repeat the layering, ending with the last piece of pastry, smooth side uppermost. Blend the remaining confectioners' sugar with sufficient cold water, a little at a time, to make a thick glacé icing. Carefully spread it over the top pastry layer. Decorate with the reserved berries, quartered or sliced if large, strawberry leaves and flowers, if available, or mint leaves, and the reserved pastry trimmings.

$\mathcal{P}$uff Pastry Slice filled with Crème Pâtissière

—————— DARTOIS ——————

*D*artois may have been named after the province of that name. On the other hand, this custard-filled pastry "bolster" may have been named in honor of Louis XVI's brother, the Comte d'Artois. Or perhaps the name comes from the late eighteenth-century vaudeville artist, Dartois.

SERVES 6–8

	Crème pâtissière
1 quantity Puff Pastry (page 123)	1 vanilla bean
1 egg white	1¾ cups milk
sugar, to sprinkle	5 egg yolks
	6 tbsp sugar
	5 tbsp flour
	pinch of salt
	1 tbsp dark rum

Prepare the crème pâtissière with the vanilla bean, milk, egg yolks, sugar, flour and salt according to the directions on page 116. Allow it to cool, then stir in the rum.

Roll out the pastry on a lightly floured surface, using a lightly floured rolling pin, to a rectangle 10 × 14 inches. Using a sharp knife, trim the edges and square the corners, then cut the rectangle in half lengthwise. Carefully transfer one piece to a dampened baking sheet, taking care to keep the shape true. Spoon the crème pâtissière over the pastry to within 1 inch of the edges. Dampen the edges with cold water, then carefully lay the second piece of pastry squarely on top. Press the edges together to seal them, then make a scallop pattern all the way around. Make 2 or 3 small holes in the top of the pastry lid with a small sharp knife. Cover loosely and chill for about 30 minutes.

Preheat the oven to 425°F.

Bake the Dartois for 20–25 minutes or until risen and golden. Beat the egg white until frothy and brush over the pastry. Sprinkle a generous layer of sugar over the top. Bake for a further 5–10 minutes or until the glaze is shiny and crisp. Carefully transfer the Dartois to a wire rack to cool.

ear Slices

——— FEUILLETES DE POIRES ———

MAKES 8

4 Comice pears
1 cup sugar
2 cups water
3 tbsp lemon juice
6 tbsp eau-de-vie de poire William
1 quantity Puff Pastry (page 123)
1 egg yolk, lightly beaten with 1 tsp water, to glaze
1 quantity Crème Frangipane (page 117)

Peel the pears, halve lengthwise and remove the cores. Poach in a syrup made from the sugar, water, lemon juice and eau-de-vie for 10–15 minutes or until just tender. Leave to cool in the syrup, then remove with a slotted spoon and leave to drain well. When drained, slice the pears.

Roll out the pastry on a lightly floured surface, using a lightly floured rolling pin, to ¼ inch thick. Trim the edges straight with a sharp knife, then cut into 8 rectangles each about 4 × 3 inches. Carefully transfer to a dampened baking sheet, taking care to keep the shapes true. Cover and chill for at least 30 minutes.

Preheat the oven to 425°F.

Brush the pastry with the egg yolk glaze and mark a pattern on the tops with the point of a sharp knife. Bake for about 7 minutes or until crisp, golden and risen. Transfer to a wire rack to cool.

Split the puff pastry rectangles horizontally into two equal layers and carefully remove any pastry that is soft. Spread a layer of crème frangipane on each of the bottom layers, arrange the sliced pears on top and cover with the top pastry layers.

$\mathscr{R}$aspberry Puffs

─────── PUITS D'AMOUR AUX FRAMBOISES ───────

It is not practical to make the small amount of crème pâtissière that is needed for this recipe so you can either reserve the required amount from some that is to be used in another recipe or you could replace the crème pâtissière with additional crème fraîche or heavy cream. However, if you do this the pastry will lose some of its special character.

MAKES 8

1 quantity Puff Pastry (page 123)
1 egg yolk, lightly beaten with 1 tsp water, to glaze
confectioners' sugar, to dredge
½ cup crème fraîche or heavy cream
2 tbsp eau-de-vie de framboise
½ cup Crème Pâtissière (page 116)
3½ cups raspberries

Roll out the pastry on a lightly floured surface, using a lightly floured rolling pin, to about ¼ inch thick. Cut into 8 rounds, each 3½–4 inches in diameter, using a plain cutter or the point of a sharp knife with a plate as a guide, or use a decorative cutter of a similar size. Carefully transfer to a dampened baking sheet making sure the shapes remain true. With the point of the knife mark lids, without cutting right through the pastry, about ½ inch in from the edge. Mark a pattern on the lid with the point of the knife. Cover and chill for 30 minutes.

Preheat the oven to 425°F.

Brush the tops of the pastry shapes with the egg yolk glaze, taking care that it does not run down the sides or into the lid markings. Bake for 12–15 minutes or until risen and golden.

Carefully lift off the lids, sift a layer of confectioners' sugar over them and place under a very hot broiler for 1–2 minutes or until glazed.

Carefully transfer the pastry cases to a wire rack and scoop out any soft dough in the centers. If necessary, return the cases to the oven for a few minutes to dry out the centers.

Whip the crème fraîche or heavy cream until it stands in soft peaks. Blend the eau-de-vie into the crème pâtissière, then fold in the whipped cream. Divide between the pastry cases, place the raspberries on top and put on the lids at a slight angle.

$\mathcal{P}$uff Pastry Slice filled with Jam

JALOUSIE

*T*his pastry is so called because its appearance resembles that of a slatted Venetian blind or
jalousie. Serve while warm but not straight from the oven as the jam will be very hot.
Jalousie can be served cold but it should be eaten on the day of making. The best accompaniments
are fromage blanc or frais and crème fraîche as their fresh, slightly "tangy" flavor provides a
good contrast to the sweet richness of the filling and pastry.

SERVES 4–5

1 quantity Puff Pastry (page 123)
5–6 tbsp jam
1 egg yolk, lightly beaten with 1 tsp water, to glaze
1 egg white, beaten until frothy
confectioners' sugar, to dredge

Roll out the pastry on a lightly floured surface, using a lightly floured rolling pin, to a large rectangle about 8 × 12 inches. Using a sharp knife, trim the edges and square the corners, then cut the dough in half lengthwise. Fold one piece in half lengthwise, then make parallel cuts from the folded edge across the pastry to within ½ inch of the outer edge.

Carefully transfer the other piece of pastry to a dampened baking sheet, making sure the shape remains true. Spread the jam over to within 1 inch of the edge. Brush the edges with cold water, then carefully lift the cut piece of pastry over the jam and lower it into place with the folded edge down the center. Unfold the pastry. Press the edges together, trim and scallop. Cover and chill for 30 minutes.

Preheat the oven to 425°F.

Brush the top of the jalousie with the egg yolk glaze, taking care that it does not run over the sides or cut edges. Bake for 25–30 minutes or until the pastry is well risen and golden brown. Brush the top with beaten egg white, sift confectioners' sugar over and place under a very hot broiler to give a fine, crisp sheen.

Carefully transfer the jalousie to a wire rack to cool.

$\mathscr{R}$*ich Almond Tartlets*

──── MIRLITONS ────

$\mathscr{M}$irlitons are small sweet tarts that are particularly associated with Normandy; those of Rouen are probably the most famous. Some Mirlitons contain butter, most have a puff pastry case, and usually they contain almonds, although the classic recipe given in "Larousse Gastronomique" does not. In some cases the egg whites are beaten separately. Mirlitons are at their best if eaten while still warm, light and risen.

MAKES 9

Puff pastry	Filling
1¼ cups all-purpose flour	3 eggs, beaten
pinch of salt	6 tbsp sugar
1 tsp lemon juice	1 cup freshly ground almonds
1½ sticks (6 oz) unsalted butter	27 blanched almond halves
	confectioners' sugar, to dredge

Make the pastry with the flour, salt, lemon juice and butter according to the directions on page 123. Cover and chill for 2 hours.

Roll out the pastry very thinly on a lightly floured surface, using a lightly floured rolling pin, and line 9 tartlet molds that are 3 inches in diameter. Cover and chill for 30 minutes.

Preheat the oven to 350–375°F, and place a baking sheet in the oven to heat.

Meanwhile, make the filling. Whisk the eggs and sugar together, and fold in the ground almonds until just evenly blended. Divide the mixture between the pastry cases so they are about three-quarters full. Place the molds on the hot baking sheet and bake for 15–18 minutes or until the filling is just beginning to set. Pull the baking sheet a little way out of the oven without removing it completely, if possible, and place 3 split almonds, equally spaced, on the top of each tartlet so they are pointing towards the center. Return the tartlets to the oven to bake for 10–15 minutes or until lightly browned and set in the center.

Carefully transfer to a wire rack. Serve warm or cold, with confectioners' sugar sifted generously over the surface just before serving.

Upside-Down Apple Tart

———— TARTE DES DEMOISELLES TATIN ————

Lamotte-Beuvran, in the Sologne area of the Loire, is the home of this upside-down apple tart. It was named after the sisters Tatin (les demoiselles Tatin), the local hotelkeepers, whose specialty it was. The sisters cooked the tart in a metal oven placed over charcoal, which was responsible for the characteristic caramelization of the sweetened buttery apple. Modern gas and electric ovens will not produce the same effect, so nowadays the apples, butter and sugar are usually browned over direct heat before being covered with pastry and baked. If using a baking pan, keep an eye on it, especially if using gas, to make sure that it doesn't burn.

SERVES 8

Puff pastry	Filling
1¼ cups all-purpose flour	1½ sticks (6 oz) unsalted butter, at
pinch of salt	room temperature
1 tsp lemon juice	1 cup sugar
1½ sticks (6 oz) unsalted butter	6 firm, tart apples, peeled, quartered
	and cored
	finely grated zest of 2 lemons

Make the pastry with the flour, salt, lemon juice and butter according to the instructions on page 123. Cover and chill for 2 hours.

Meanwhile, make the filling. Coat the bottom and sides of a heavy 9 inch skillet or sauteuse that can go in the oven (check the material of the handle), or a thick-bottomed 9 inch baking pan, enameled cast iron dish or even a paella pan, with a thick layer of butter. Sprinkle over about two-thirds of the sugar. Cut each apple quarter in half lengthwise and arrange them in concentric circles in the pan. Sprinkle the remaining sugar and the lemon zest over, then scatter over the remaining butter, cut into small pieces. Cook over a high heat for about 15 minutes or until the apples are tender and the butter and sugar thickened and turned golden brown. Remove from the heat and allow to cool, removing a little of the liquid if there is a lot.

Roll out the pastry on a lightly floured surface, using a lightly floured rolling pin, to a round about 9½ inches in diameter. Prick it well with the tines of a fork, lay it on a dampened baking sheet, cover and chill for 30 minutes.

Preheat the oven to 425°F.

Cover the apples with the pastry. Bake for 12–15 minutes, then lower the oven temperature to 350°F and continue to bake for a further 10–12 minutes or until the pastry is well risen and crisp.

Leave to cool for a few minutes, then invert on to a hot plate and serve warm.

Caramelized Apple Tart

—— GALETTE FINE AUX POMMES CARAMELISEES ——

*I*n this Normandy specialty, soft apples are sandwiched between a crisp pastry base and a crunchy caramel top. Use an apple that has a slightly sharp flavor, to provide a contrast to the sweet butteriness, and that will retain its shape when cooked.

SERVES 6

½ quantity Puff Pastry (page 123)
2 tbsp sugar
4 tart apples, cored and thinly sliced
3 tbsp unsalted butter, diced
1 tsp clear honey
4 tbsp apple juice
2 tbsp Calvados

Roll out the pastry on a lightly floured surface, using a lightly floured rolling pin, to a round about ⅛ inch thick. Very carefully transfer the pastry round to a heavy, dampened baking sheet, making sure that the shape remains true. Cover and chill for 30 minutes.

Preheat the oven to 425°F.

Sprinkle the sugar over the pastry, then arrange the slices of apple, overlapping each other, in neat concentric circles on top. Scatter the butter over the surface. Bake for 20–30 minutes or until the pastry is golden and the apples lightly caramelized.

Meanwhile, warm the honey very slightly if necessary so that it becomes just runny enough to blend smoothly with the apple juice and Calvados.

Carefully transfer the pastry to a serving plate and immediately spoon the apple juice mixture evenly over the surface. Serve immediately.

$\mathcal{P}$uff Pastry Hearts

PALMIERS

$\mathcal{P}$almiers can be eaten plain or sandwiched together in pairs with whipped cream and dredged with confectioners' sugar. They can also be made with puff pastry trimmings.

MAKES ABOUT 24

½ quantity Puff Pastry (page 123)

sugar, to sprinkle

Sprinkle sugar liberally over a work surface, then roll out the pastry on it to a rectangle approximately 6 × 18 inches. Sprinkle sugar over the surface of the dough. Fold the bottom third of the dough up and the top two thirds down over it. Turn the dough round through 45° and roll it out again. Sprinkle once more with sugar and fold as before. Cover and chill for 30 minutes.

Sprinkle the work surface with sugar again, sprinkle sugar over the dough and roll it out to a rectangle ⅙ inch thick. Using a sharp knife, trim the edges. Mark a very faint line lengthwise down the center of the dough. Fold the long sides in half lengthwise so that they meet in the center, then fold them lengthwise in half again. Press very lightly with a rolling pin, then fold one side over the other. Using a sharp knife, cut across into ½ inch slices. Transfer to a dampened baking sheet, placing them cut side downward. Leave room between them to allow for spreading. Cover and chill for 30 minutes.

Preheat the oven to 425°F.

Bake the palmiers for 8–10 minutes or until well risen and just turning golden brown. Carefully turn the palmiers over using a slotted spatula and return them to the oven to bake for a further 5 minutes or so to brown the other side.

Transfer to a wire rack carefully – they will be very hot – and leave to cool.

Illustrated on page 50

Almond-Filled Pastry Cake

———— GATEAU DE PITHIVIERS FEUILLETE ————

*T*his deliciously rich pastry, unchanged from at least the beginning of the nineteenth century, bears
the name of a small town about 80 kilometers south of Paris, in the Orléanais. However, there is
some doubt about whether this was, in fact, its original birthplace.

SERVES 6–8

	Filling
1 quantity Puff Pastry (page 123)	*Filling*
1 egg yolk, lightly beaten with 1 tsp cold water, to glaze	1 cup freshly ground almonds
	6 tbsp sugar
confectioners' sugar, to dredge	6 tbsp unsalted butter, softened
	2 egg yolks, beaten
	2 tbsp dark rum

For the filling, pound the almonds with the sugar to make a paste, using a pestle and mortar, then spoon
the paste into a bowl and work in the butter followed by the egg yolks and rum. Cover and chill very well.

Divide the pastry into two portions, one slightly larger than the other. Roll out the smaller portion on a
lightly floured surface, using a lightly floured rolling pin, to a round about 9½ inches in diameter. Trim the
edges and carefully transfer to a dampened baking sheet, making sure the shape remains true.

Roll out the other piece of pastry to a similar round and trim the edges. Place the almond filling on the
first round, leaving a border of about 1 inch clear all the way around. Brush the border with the egg yolk
glaze. Place the second round of pastry centrally over the filling and press the pastry edges together to seal
them. Form a scallop effect around the edge and make a small slit in the center of the lid. With the point of a
sharp knife, starting at the center and working to the edge, score the surface of the pastry (without cutting
right through) in curved, half-moon shaped lines. This will give the traditional appearance. Brush the top
with egg yolk glaze, avoiding the scored lines, cover and chill for 30 minutes.

Preheat the oven to 425°F.

Bake for about 20 minutes, then lower the oven temperature to 400°F and bake for a further 15 minutes or
so or until the pastry is risen and golden brown. Sprinkle confectioners' sugar over the surface and place the
pastry under a very hot broiler for 1–2 minutes to glaze. Carefully transfer to a wire rack to cool slightly
before serving.

Illustrated on page 51

Puff Pastry Hearts

Almond-Filled Pastry Cake

Choux Pastry

Choux Pastry Gâteau

GATEAU ST HONORE

This gâteau is named after the seventh century Bishop of Amiens, Honoré, who became the patron saint of bakers and pastrycooks because, according to the story, a loaf of bread was presented to him by a divine hand on one occasion when he was celebrating mass.

SERVES 8

1 quantity Pâte Sucrée, made with 1½ tbsp vanilla sugar (page 121)	6 tbsp sugar
	5 tbsp flour
double quantity Choux Pastry (page 122)	pinch of salt
	6 egg whites
1 egg, lightly beaten with 1 tsp water, to glaze	*Filling*
	about ½ cup heavy cream
Crème St Honoré	1 tbsp vanilla sugar
1 vanilla bean, split	*Caramel*
2 cups milk	1 cup sugar
6 egg yolks	½ cup water

Preheat the oven to 400°F. Butter a baking sheet.

Roll out the pâte sucrée on a lightly floured surface, using a lightly floured rolling pin to a round about 9–10 inches in diameter that is ¼ inch thick. Carefully transfer the pastry to the baking sheet, making sure the shape remains true. Prick lightly with a fork, cover and chill for 30 minutes.

Brush a ½ inch wide border around the edge of the pastry round with the egg glaze. Spoon the choux pastry into a pastry bag fitted with a ¾ inch plain tube and pipe a ring of choux pastry on to the egg-glazed border. Brush the top of the choux pastry with egg glaze, then bake for about 25 minutes or until the choux is risen and both the choux ring and pastry base are brown.

Immediately after the pastry is taken from the oven, make several small slits in the side of the choux ring and return to the oven to bake for about 3 minutes longer. Transfer to a wire rack to cool.

Pipe approximately 15 balls the size of largish walnuts on to the baking sheet, spacing them slightly apart to allow them room to spread. Brush the tops of the balls with egg glaze and bake for 15–18 minutes or until puffed and golden. Make a small hole in the bottom of each bun, then return them to the oven to bake for a few minutes longer. Transfer to a wire rack to cool.

For the crème St Honoré, add the vanilla bean to the milk and heat in a heavy-bottomed saucepan to just below simmering point. Remove from the heat, cover and leave to infuse for 20 minutes. Beat the egg yolks with two-thirds of the sugar, then mix in the flour and salt. Remove the vanilla bean from the milk. Bring the milk to a boil, then slowly pour onto the egg mixture, whisking continuously. Pour back into the rinsed pan and heat gently, whisking, until the mixture comes to the boil. Still whisking, simmer the custard for 2 minutes, then pass through a sieve.

Beat the egg whites until stiff, then beat in the remaining sugar and continue to beat until glossy. Quickly stir one-third of the egg whites into the hot custard, then lightly and quickly fold the custard into the remaining egg whites until just evenly blended. Leave to cool to room temperature.

For the filling, whip the cream until it begins to stiffen. Sprinkle the sugar over and whip again until soft peaks form. Spoon into a pastry bag fitted with a small tube and use to fill the choux buns through the holes in the bottom. Reserve the remaining cream in the bag for decoration.

For the caramel, gently heat the sugar and water in a heavy-bottomed saucepan, stirring until dissolved, then bring to a boil and boil, without stirring, until a caramel color. Remove from the heat and place the saucepan in a saucepan of warm water to keep warm.

Spear each choux bun in turn on a fine skewer, dip the bottom into the caramel and place around the top of the choux ring. Using a metal spoon, trickle the remaining caramel over the tops of the choux buns. Fill the center of the pastry case with the crème St Honoré and decorate with the reserved cream.

Illustrated on page 54

$\mathcal{D}$eep-Fried Choux Balls

—————————— PETS-DE-NONNE ——————————

*T*hese pastries are associated with the convent at Baume-les-Dames, in the mountainous *countryside of Franche-Comté. The nuns there also produced first class wafers and cookies as well as these crunchy light morsels.*

SERVES 4

1 quantity Choux Pastry (page 122)
orange flower water, to taste (optional)
sugar, to coat

Heat a deep-fat fryer half filled with oil to 350°F.

If liked, beat a few drops of orange flower water into the choux pastry to flavor it. Dip a teaspoon into the hot oil, then scoop out a teaspoonful of the pastry and carefully push it into the oil, using another teaspoon. Add another 4 or 5 spoonfuls of pastry in the same way, increasing the heat beneath the pan slightly to compensate for the cooling of the oil as the pastry is added. The temperature of the oil can rise to about 375°F but no more. Cook the pastry balls for about 3 minutes or until puffed up and golden. Remove the balls using a slotted spoon and drain them on paper towels, then roll them in sugar to coat well in an even crunchy layer. Keep warm in a very low oven while cooking the remainder.

Eat the pets-de-nonne while they are still warm.

Choux Pastry Gâteau

Eclairs

——— ECLAIRS ———

MAKES ABOUT 16

1 quantity Choux Pastry (page 122)	*Icing*
1 quantity Crème Pâtissière (page 116)	3 tbsp vanilla sugar
	5 tbsp water
1 oz good quality milk chocolate, broken (optional)	4 oz semisweet chocolate, broken
	1 tbsp unsalted butter, diced

Preheat the oven to 400°F. Dampen a large baking sheet.

Spoon the choux pastry into a pastry bag fitted with a ½ inch plain tube. Pipe in straight lengths, about 3–3½ inches long, on the baking sheet, leaving room between them to allow for expansion. Bake for 20–25 minutes or until risen, firm and brown. Immediately the éclairs are taken from the oven, make a slit in the side of each one. Return them to the oven to bake for 2–3 minutes longer. Transfer to a wire rack to cool.

Spoon the crème pâtissière into a pastry bag fitted with a small tube and fill the éclairs through the slits in the sides.

For the icing, gently heat the sugar in the water, stirring until it dissolves, then bring to a boil quickly and boil, without stirring, for 2 minutes.

Meanwhile, melt the semisweet chocolate in a small bowl placed over a saucepan of hot but not boiling water, stirring occasionally. Stir in the sugar syrup until the chocolate is smooth. Remove from the heat and stir in the butter until melted.

Dip the tops of the éclairs in the icing and allow the excess to drain off. Leave the éclairs on a wire rack until the icing is set.

Melt the milk chocolate in a bowl placed over a saucepan of hot but not boiling water. Put into a small wax paper pastry bag with the point snipped off (or a small pastry bag fitted with a small plain tube) and pipe a zig-zag pattern on the icing. Leave to set before serving.

Choux Pastry Ring with Praline Filling

———— GATEAU PARIS–BREST ————

*R*ich buttercream is the classic filling for a Gâteau Paris–Brest, but lighter crème pâtissière is also acceptable.

SERVES 6–8

	Praline
1 quantity Choux Pastry (page 122)	½ cup sugar
1 egg, lightly beaten with 1 tsp water, to glaze	⅔ cup shelled almonds
¼ cup slivered almonds	*Rich buttercream*
confectioners' sugar, to dredge	6 tbsp sugar
	5 tbsp water
	3 egg yolks
	1½ sticks (6 oz) unsalted butter, softened

Preheat the oven to 400°F. Dampen a baking sheet. Draw a 7–8 inch circle on a sheet of parchment paper so that the mark shows through the other side. Turn the sheet over and place on the baking sheet.

Spoon the choux pastry into a pastry bag fitted with a ¾ inch plain tube. Pipe a thick ring about 1 inch high on the parchment paper, following the drawn circle. Lightly brush the egg glaze over the ring and sprinkle on the slivered almonds. Bake for 30–35 minutes or until risen, browned and firm.

Immediately after the ring is taken from the oven, split it in half horizontally. Carefully scoop out any soft pastry in the center and return the two halves of the ring to the oven to bake for about 3 minutes longer. Transfer the ring to a wire rack to cool.

Make the praline with the sugar and almonds according to the instructions on page 9. Grind finely.

Make the buttercream with the sugar, water, egg yolks and butter according to the instructions on page 118.

Stir the praline into the buttercream. Spoon it into a pastry bag fitted with a large star tube and pipe into the bottom half of the pastry ring to fill it. Place the other half of the ring gently on top – the filling should be clearly visible around the sides. Sift confectioners' sugar over the top.

Choux Puffs with Orange Filling

———— CHOUX A L'ORANGE ————

The orange filling can be prepared in advance to the stage where the candied peel is added, and kept in an airtight container in the refrigerator for several days. Bring it to room temperature to soften before folding in the cream.

MAKES 8

1 quantity Choux Pastry (page 122)	*Glaze*
chopped orange segments, to	¼ cup sugar
decorate	⅔ cup water
Filling	pared zest of 1 orange
1 tbsp unsalted butter, diced	
5 tbsp sugar	
2 egg yolks, beaten	
finely grated zest and strained juice	
of 1 large or 2 small oranges	
3–4 tbsp chopped, candied	
orange peel	
⅔ cup heavy cream	

Preheat the oven to 400°F. Dampen a baking sheet.

Spoon the choux pastry into a pastry bag fitted with a ¾ inch plain tube and pipe large buns, spaced well apart, on the baking sheet. Bake for about 25 minutes or until risen, browned and firm.

Immediately after the buns are taken from the oven split them open. Carefully scoop out any soft pastry and return them to the oven to bake for about 3 minutes longer. Transfer the buns to a wire rack and leave to cool.

For the filling, gently heat the butter and sugar in a bowl placed over a saucepan of hot water, stirring with a wooden spoon, until the butter has melted. Stir in the egg yolks and orange zest and juice and cook, stirring, until the custard thickens and coats the back of the spoon. Remove from the heat, stir in the candied peel and pour into a bowl. Leave to cool, stirring occasionally.

For the glaze, gently heat the sugar and water in a heavy-bottomed saucepan, stirring until the sugar has dissolved. Add the orange zest, bring to a boil and boil steadily, without stirring, for 10–15 minutes. Discard the orange zest, and remove the pan from the heat.

Whip the cream until stiff, then gently and lightly fold in the orange custard. Use to fill the choux buns. Brush the tops with the glaze and decorate with pieces of orange.

Choux Hearts with Peaches and Cream

—————— COEURS AUX PECHES ——————

MAKES 8

1 quantity Choux Pastry (page 122)
1 egg, lightly beaten with 1 tsp water, to glaze
3 ripe peaches
⅔ cup crème fraîche or heavy cream
¼ lb fresh cream cheese
1 egg white
1½ tbsp vanilla sugar
6 tbsp Apricot Glaze, made with a little orange liqueur (page 9)
candied peach slices, to decorate

Preheat the oven to 400°F. Dampen a baking sheet.

Spoon the pastry into a pastry bag fitted with a ½ inch plain tube and pipe heart shapes about 2½–3 inches long on the baking sheet. Brush the tops with the egg glaze. Bake for about 20 minutes or until risen, crisp and browned.

Immediately the hearts are removed from the oven, split each open horizontally along one edge and carefully scoop out any soft dough. Return to the oven to bake for a few minutes longer, then leave to cool on a wire rack.

Dip the peaches individually in boiling water for about 20 seconds, then peel them. Cut them in half, remove the pits and chop the flesh.

Blend about 2 tbsp of the crème fraîche or heavy cream into the cream cheese. Whip the remaining crème fraîche or cream until it stands in soft peaks, then fold it into the cheese. Beat the egg white until peaks form, sprinkle the sugar over the surface and beat again until shiny. Fold into the cheese mixture. Fold in the chopped peaches.

Divide the filling between the hearts. Brush the tops with apricot glaze and decorate with the candied peach slices immediately.

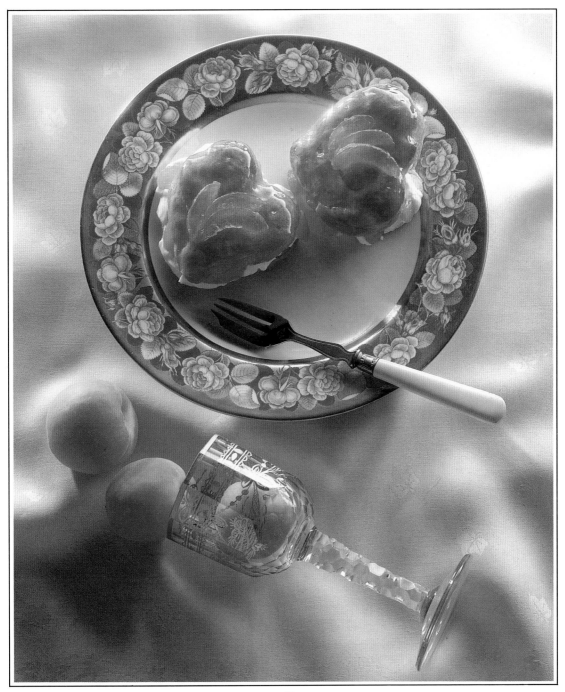

Choux Bun Pyramid

CROQUEMBOUCHE

"Croquembouche" is a name that can be given to all types of pâtisserie that crunch and crumble in the mouth, although it is normally thought of as being a pointed tower of small choux buns mounted on a pâte sucrée base. This Croquembouche was created in the nineteenth century when it was fashionable for large amounts of food to be displayed on large tables – if a dish was to make an impact, it had to be big, preferably tall, and stunning. Such an elaborate pièce montée is no longer so popular today, and the traditional decoration of spun sugar requires a skilled hand, so this recipe is a simplified version. Master pâtissiers constructed their pyramid around a large metal cone, which was then removed. This recipe uses an ordinary bowl.

SERVES 6–8

Pâte sucrée	Filling
⅔ cup all-purpose flour	2½ cups heavy cream
small pinch of salt	2 tbsp Cognac
4 tbsp unsalted butter, diced	2 tbsp sifted vanilla confectioners'
1 small egg yolk	sugar
2 tbsp sugar	about 3 cups prepared fresh fruit
Choux pastry	such as strawberries, raspberries,
¾ cup all-purpose flour	peaches, nectarines or cherries
pinch of salt	1 cup sugar
5 tbsp unsalted butter, diced	⅔ cup water
¾ cup water	crystallized or fresh
3–4 eggs, beaten	flowers, to decorate

Prepare the pâte sucrée with the flour, salt, butter, egg yolk and sugar according to the instructions on page 121.

Roll out the pastry on a lightly floured surface, using a lightly floured rolling pin, to a 7 inch round. Carefully transfer to a baking sheet, making sure the shape remains true. Prick the pastry with the tines of a fork, cover and chill for 30 minutes.

Preheat the oven to 400°F. Bake the pastry round for 15–20 minutes or until a light golden color. Transfer to a wire rack and leave to cool.

Prepare the choux pastry with the flour, salt, butter, water and eggs according to the directions on page 122.

Dampen two baking sheets. Spoon the choux pastry into a pastry bag fitted with a small plain tube and pipe small balls on the baking sheets. Bake for about 20 minutes or until risen and golden. Immediately after the buns are removed from the oven, make a hole in the bottom of each and leave to cool on a wire rack.

Whip the cream until it forms soft peaks. Spoon about half into a pastry bag fitted with a small, plain tube and use most of it to fill the buns through the holes in the bottoms. Lightly whisk the Cognac and confectioners' sugar into the remaining cream, and fold in the fruit.

Gently heat the sugar and water in a thick-bottomed saucepan, stirring until the sugar has dissolved. Bring to a boil and boil, without stirring, until the syrup turns golden brown. Place the saucepan in a pan of hot water to keep the caramel warm without further cooking.

Oil a 7 inch diameter bowl (about 5 inches high) and place upside down on a work surface.

Spear each bun in turn on a fine skewer and dip in the caramel. Arrange them in three tiers of decreasing size around the bottom part of the bowl. Leave the caramel coating on the balls to set.

Spoon the cream and fruit onto the center of the pastry round, mounding it up. Very gently lift the set choux buns off their bowl and place over the cream filling. Dip the remaining buns in the caramel and stack them on the other buns to form a dome-shape, enclosing the filling. Spoon any remaining caramel over the gâteau so that it trickles down the sides. Pipe the remaining cream at random in the spaces between the buns, and decorate with crystallized or fresh flowers.

Illustrated on page 62

Choux Bun Pyramid

Small Éclairs with Kirsch-Flavored Filling

SALAMBOS

It is traditional to use glacé cherries to decorate each Salambo, but if fresh cherries are available I would prefer to break with tradition and suggest you use these instead.

MAKES ABOUT 18

1 quantity Choux Pastry (page 122)
1 egg, lightly beaten with 1 tsp water, to glaze
about 3 tbsp sliced glacé cherries
2 tbsp Kirsch
1 quantity Crème Pâtissière (page 116)
1 quantity Fondant (page 119)

Preheat the oven to 400°F. Butter two baking sheets.

Spoon the choux pastry into a pastry bag fitted with a ½ inch plain tube and pipe in 1¼ inch lengths on the baking sheets. Brush the tops with the egg glaze. Bake for about 25 minutes or until risen, browned and firm. Immediately the pastries are removed from the oven, make a hole in the side of each. Transfer to a wire rack and leave to cool completely.

Marinate the glacé cherries in half of the Kirsch.

Flavor the crème pâtissière with the remaining Kirsch and leave to stand for a short while to allow the flavors to blend.

Spoon the crème pâtissière into a pastry bag fitted with a ¼ inch plain tube, and fill each choux shape through the hole in the side.

Drain the cherries.

Gently warm the fondant in a bowl placed over a saucepan of hot water. Dip the top of each éclair in fondant to coat, and decorate with slices of glacé cherry.

Meringues

Nut Meringue Gâteau

DACQUOISE

Dacquoise is named after the town of Dax, in the south of the Landes. The simple cream filling is sometimes replaced by a butter-enriched crème pâtissière flavored with praline and perhaps hazelnuts (filberts) as well.

SERVES 6

⅔ cup freshly ground almonds	*Filling*
⅔ cups freshly ground hazelnuts (filberts)	1¼ cups crème fraîche or heavy cream
2 tsp cornstarch	1 tbsp vanilla sugar
4 egg whites	1½ cups strawberries
⅔ cup vanilla superfine sugar	
confectioners' sugar, to dredge	

Draw an 8 inch circle on two sheets of parchment paper so the markings show through the paper. Place the sheets with the markings on the underside on two large baking sheets. Preheat the oven to 275°F.

Mix the almonds, hazelnuts and cornstarch together. Beat the egg whites until stiff. Sprinkle over 2 tbsp of the sugar and beat for about 30 seconds longer or until the whites just become glossy. Add another 2 tbsp of sugar and beat again for about 30 seconds or until just becoming glossy, then very lightly fold in the remaining sugar using a large metal spoon. Fold in the almond mixture. When just evenly combined, spread inside the marked circles on the baking sheets. Bake for about 50 minutes or until crisp, dry and lightly browned.

Carefully remove the meringue rounds from the paper and transfer to a wire rack to cool.

For the filling, whip the crème fraîche or cream until it begins to thicken. Add the sugar and whip until the cream stands in soft peaks. Slice the strawberries if large and reserve a few for decoration.

Spread two-thirds of the cream on one of the meringue rounds. Cover with strawberries. Place the other meringue round on top. Place a paper doily on the surface and sift a thick layer of confectioners' sugar over. Lift the doily away cleanly to leave a pattern on the surface. Decorate the top of the Dacquoise with the remaining cream and reserved strawberries.

$\mathcal{M}$*eringue Basket*

VACHERIN

This is said to have been a favorite of Marie Antoinette, and she is even reputed to have made vacherins herself, but as it is quite a complicated dish this seems unlikely.

SERVES 6–8

8 egg whites
4 cups vanilla confectioners' sugar, sifted
2 cups heavy cream
1 lb (3–4 cups) prepared fresh fruit

Draw a 7 inch circle on four sheets of parchment paper so the marking shows through. Line baking sheets with the paper, with the marked side downward. Preheat the oven to the lowest possible setting.

Beat 4 of the egg whites until stiff in a large bowl. Place the bowl over a saucepan of gently simmering water so that it fits snugly without touching the water. Gradually beat in half of the sugar until the mixture is very thick. Remove the bowl from the heat and continue to beat for 2–3 minutes. Spoon the meringue into a pastry bag fitted with a ½ inch plain tube. Pipe a spiral of meringue, starting at the center, to fill one of the marked circles. Smooth the surface gently with a spatula. Pipe a ring of meringue around each of the remaining marked circles.

Bake the meringue for about 2 hours or until dry and crisp but still white. Keep an eye on the meringues to make sure they do not color – if necessary, prop the oven door open with the handle of a wooden spoon.

Carefully transfer the meringues to a wire rack to cool.

Line a baking sheet with a fresh sheet of parchment paper.

Prepare a second batch of meringue in the same way as the first using the remaining egg whites and sugar.

Place the solid round of cooked meringue on the baking sheet. Stack the rings on top using some of the second batch of meringue to "stick" them together. Spoon the remainder of the meringue into a pastry bag fitted with a plain tube and, working from the bottom upwards, pipe in straight vertical lines up the sides of the basket all the way around. Pipe short horizontal lines around the basket to resemble the "weave." Pipe scrolls, shells or rosettes around the top edge. Bake again for about 1½ hours.

Carefully transfer the vacherin to a wire rack to cool, then remove the lining paper.

Whip the cream until it stands in soft peaks. Layer the cream and fruit in the vacherin, forming it into a mound. Serve within 3–4 hours of assembling.

Illustrated on pages 66–7

Meringue Basket

$\mathcal{N}$ut Meringue layered with Praline, Noix and Chocolate

———— MARJOLAINE ————

$\mathcal{N}$*oix is a liqueur made from walnuts. If you are unable to buy it, Amaretto, which is made from almonds, although Italian, could be used instead.*

SERVES 6–8

½ cup freshly ground, lightly toasted almonds
½ cup freshly ground, lightly toasted hazelnuts (filberts)
⅔ cup vanilla superfine sugar
2 tsp cornstarch
4 egg whites
1 quantity Crème Pâtissière (page 116)
1 stick unsalted butter, softened
3 tbsp Noix
3–4 tbsp Praline (page 9)
⅔ cup heavy cream
6 oz bittersweet chocolate, chopped
2 tbsp Cognac
fine chocolate caraque, to decorate (optional)

Draw four rectangles, approximately 7 × 4 inches, on parchment paper so the markings show through, then lay the paper on baking sheets with the markings underneath. Preheat the oven to 375°F.

In a mortar, grind the nuts finely with ½ cup of the sugar and the cornstarch. Beat the egg whites until stiff, sprinkle the remaining sugar over and beat for another 30 seconds or so until shiny. Using a metal spoon, gently and quickly fold in the nut mixture until just evenly blended.

Divide the mixture between the baking sheets, spreading evenly inside the drawn rectangles and smoothing the surface with a spatula. Bake for about 20 minutes or until an even light brown. Carefully remove from the paper and leave on a wire rack to cool.

Gradually beat half of the crème pâtissière into the butter, adding the Noix toward the end. Reserve a little of the mixture for decoration; cover and chill the remainder until it reaches a spreadable consistency (the reserved portion needs to be at a pipeable consistency). Add the praline to the remaining crème pâtissière. Cover and chill for about 1 hour.

Bring the cream to a boil. Remove from the heat, stir in the chocolate and continue to stir until the chocolate has melted and the mixture is completely smooth. Stir in the Cognac. Leave to cool. Reserve a little of the chocolate cream at room temperature for decoration. Chill the remainder of the mixture until it reaches a spreadable consistency.

Place one of the meringue layers on a serving plate and spread the chilled chocolate cream over. Place another meringue layer on top and cover with two-thirds to three-quarters of the Noix-flavored crème pâtissière. Put on a third meringue layer and spread this with the praline-flavored crème pâtissière. Top with the last meringue layer.

Spoon the reserved Noix-flavored crème pâtissière and chocolate cream into separate pastry bags fitted with star tubes, and decorate the top of the Marjolaine together with the chocolate caraque, if using. Chill for several hours before serving.

Illustrated on page 71

$\mathscr{S}mall\ Meringues\ with\ Chocolate$

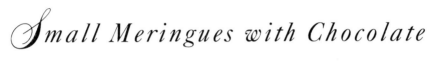

——— PETITES MERINGUES AU CHOCOLAT ———

$\mathscr{J}$ust how many meringues you make will depend on the size you make them, but they look best if they are quite small. Similarly, it is difficult to be exact about the amount of chocolate and cream that are needed so the quantities below are just a guide.

MAKES ABOUT 40

½ quantity Italian Meringue (page 125)
3 oz semisweet chocolate, chopped
¼ cup heavy cream
½ tsp sifted confectioners' sugar
1 tsp Cognac

Line two large baking sheets with parchment paper.

Preheat the oven to the lowest possible setting.

Spoon the meringue into a pastry bag fitted with a ¼ inch plain tube and pipe about 80 small blobs on the baking sheets. Bake for about 1½ hours or until crisp on the outside but very slightly softer in the center and still white. Carefully transfer the meringues to a wire rack to cool.

Melt the chocolate in a bowl placed over a saucepan of hot but not boiling water. Stir until smooth, then remove the saucepan from the heat. Dip the tops of half of the meringues in the chocolate. Leave them, chocolate side uppermost, to set.

Whip the cream with the sugar until just stiff and flavor with the Cognac. Use to sandwich plain meringues with chocolate-topped ones. Serve in small paper candy (bonbon) cases, if liked.

Illustrated on page 70

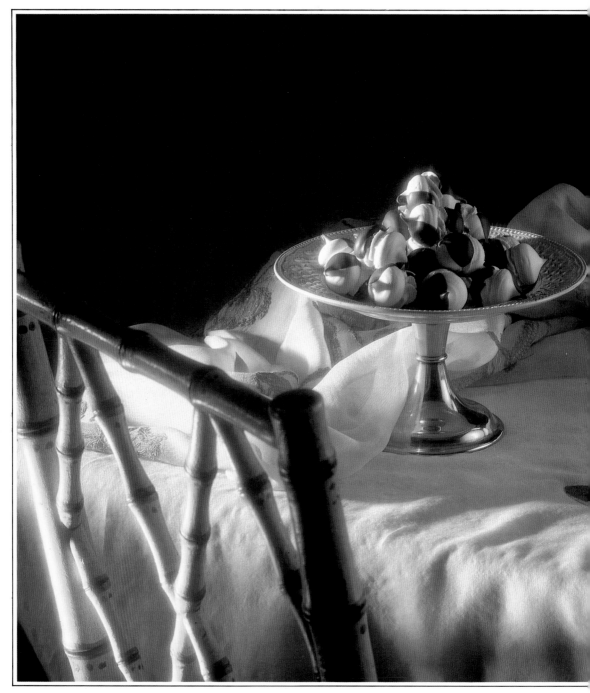

Small Meringues with Chocolate

Nut Meringue layered with Praline, Noix and Chocolate

Fruit-Filled Meringue Nests

——————— MERINGUES AUX FRUITS ———————

This particular recipe, which combines moist, tangy fruit, luscious soft cream, preferably with the "bite" of Cognac, bitter chocolate and sweet crisp meringue, is quite irresistible.

MAKES 6–8

1 quantity Italian Meringue (page 125)
about 1½–2 oz bittersweet chocolate, chopped
1½ cups crème fraîche or heavy cream
2 tbsp Cognac (optional)
about 2 cups prepared fruit such as strawberries, raspberries, cherries, pears or peaches

Draw six to eight 4 inch circles on a large piece of parchment paper so the markings show through the other side, then place on a baking sheet with the marked side downward. Preheat the oven to the lowest possible setting.

Spoon the meringue into a pastry bag fitted with a ½ inch plain tube and pipe in spirals, starting in the center, to fill the marked circles. Pipe 3 rings, one above the other, around the outside of each round to make a basket.

Bake on the lowest shelf in the oven for 4–4½ hours or until crisp and white on the outside but still soft in the center. If the baskets begin to color, prop open the oven door with the handle of a wooden spoon. Carefully transfer to a wire rack to cool.

Melt the chocolate in a small bowl placed over hot but not boiling water, stirring until smooth. Remove from the heat and cool slightly, then carefully brush a thin layer over the insides of each meringue basket.

Whip the crème fraîche or cream until it stands in soft peaks. Whip in the Cognac.

Place some of the fruit in the baskets, pipe in swirls of cream and decorate with the remaining fruit.

*H*azelnut Praline Meringue *C*ake

LE SUCCESS

SERVES 8

		Praline	
4 egg whites		½ cup shelled hazelnuts	
1⅓ cups freshly ground hazelnuts (filberts)		5 tbsp sugar	
2 tsp cornstarch			
½ cup superfine sugar			
1 quantity Rich Buttercream (page 118)			
blanched hazelnuts, (filberts), to decorate			

Draw an 8 inch circle on two sheets of parchment paper so the markings show through. Lay on two baking sheets with the marked side downward. Preheat the oven to 250°F.

Beat the egg whites until stiff. Mix the hazelnuts, cornstarch and all but 2 tbsp of the sugar together. Beat the remaining sugar into the egg whites for about 30 seconds or until glossy, then lightly and quickly fold in the hazelnut mixture. Spoon into a pastry bag fitted with a ½ inch plain tube. Starting at the center of the drawn circles, pipe a spiral of meringue to fill each one.

Bake for about 45 minutes or until the meringues are crisp, dry and just beginning to brown. Trim the meringue rounds to neat shapes while they are still warm, then carefully remove the paper and transfer the rounds to wire racks to cool.

Make the praline with the hazelnuts and sugar according to the instructions on page 9. Crush about one-third of the praline coarsely, and the remainder finely. Mix half to two-thirds of the buttercream with the finely crushed praline.

Sandwich the meringue layers together with the praline-flavored buttercream. Using a palette knife, spread most of the unflavored buttercream around the sides and smoothly over the top of the gâteau. Press the coarsely crushed praline onto the sides. Spoon the remaining buttercream into a pastry bag fitted with a star tube and use to decorate the top. Finish with whole hazelnuts.

Chestnut Meringue Cake

—— GATEAU AUX MARRONS ——

At one time, chestnuts were a staple food for the poor in many areas of France. They would be dried for eating whole and grinding into flour to make breads, cakes and pastries. Nowadays, particularly in the Ardèche, they are sold whole and puréed in cans and made into expensive marrons glacés.

SERVES 8

1½ quantities Italian Meringue (page 125)	*Filling*
	1¼ cups unsweetened chestnut purée, sieved
	2 tbsp vanilla sugar
	1½ cups heavy cream
	halves or pieces of marrons glacés and chocolate leaves, to decorate

Draw two 8 inch circles on one or two sheets of parchment paper, depending on the size of your baking sheets, so the markings show through, then lay the paper on the baking sheet(s) with the marked side downward. Line another baking sheet with parchment paper. Preheat the oven to 225°F.

Spoon about one-third of the meringue into a pastry bag fitted with a 1 inch star tube and pipe eight shell shapes on the unmarked parchment paper. Spoon the remaining meringue into a pastry bag fitted with a ½ inch plain tube and pipe in spirals to fill the marked circles, starting at the centers.

Bake for about 1 hour or until the meringues are dry and crisp and only lightly tinged with color. If they begin to color too much, prop open the oven door with the handle of a wooden spoon. Change the position of the baking sheets about halfway through the baking.

Carefully remove the meringues from the paper and transfer to a wire rack to cool.

For the filling, beat the chestnut purée with the sugar until very smooth, then spoon some into a pastry bag fitted with a star tube. Whip the cream until it stands in soft peaks. Fold most of the cream into the remaining chestnut purée and use to sandwich the meringue layers together. Place the meringue shells on top, securing them with a little cream, and decorate the top of the gâteau with the reserved chestnut purée, the reserved cream, marrons glacés and a few chocolate leaves.

Cakes

Breton Butter Cake

— GATEAU BRETON —

A simple, yet buttery cake, this is found all over Brittany, for sale in markets and on street corners, to be eaten with a glass of cider. It is recognizable by the lattice design.

SERVES 6–8

3 cups cake flour
¾ cup sugar
6 egg yolks
2 sticks (8 oz) unsalted butter, at room temperature, diced

Butter a 9 inch tart ring placed on a baking sheet, or a tart pan with a removable base. Preheat the oven to 375°F.

Sift the flour onto a cold work surface. Mix in the sugar, then make a well in the center. Beat 5 of the egg yolks lightly together with a fork and pour into the well. Add the butter, then work the two together with your fingertips until evenly blended. Using a cold metal palette knife, fold and cut the flour/sugar mixture into the egg/butter mixture. When the ingredients are just coming together, use your fingers and the heel of your hand to work them gently until they are just forming into a smooth dough. When the mixture becomes too sticky to handle, use a palette knife again.

Press the mixture into the tart ring or pan in an even, smooth layer. Glaze the top with the remaining egg yolk lightly beaten with 1 tsp water, then trace a lattice pattern on it using the tines of a fork. Bake for about 20 minutes, then lower the temperature to 350°F and bake for a further 30 minutes or until the top is golden and firm to the touch.

Leave to cool slightly before unmolding onto a wire rack to cool completely.

$\mathcal{L}$ight Sponge Cake

—— BISCUIT DE SAVOIE ——

Biscuit de Savoie is similar to Biscuit (page 124), but it is made extra light by the inclusion of potato flour (or cornstarch if potato flour is not available). It is flavored most often with orange flower water, but vanilla extract or finely grated lemon zest are also sometimes used.

SERVES 4–6

4 eggs, separated
½ cup sugar
½ cup cake flour
½ cup potato flour or cornstarch
pinch of salt
2 tbsp unsalted butter, melted
orange flower water, a few drops of vanilla extract
or the finely grated zest of 1 lemon
¼ cup sliced almonds
confectioners' sugar, to dredge

Butter an 8 inch springform or loose-bottomed cake pan, line the bottom with buttered parchment paper and sprinkle with sugar. Preheat the oven to 350°F.

Beat the egg yolks and half of the sugar together until thick and pale and the mixture leaves a trail on the surface when the beater is lifted from it.

Beat the egg whites until soft peaks are formed. Add the remaining sugar and beat again until the mixture is stiff and shiny.

Sift the flours and salt together. Using a large metal spoon, fold the dry ingredients into the egg yolk mixture very gently and quickly, in two or three batches, alternately with the beaten egg whites. Add the butter and flavoring with the last addition of egg white.

Pour into the cake pan, tap the pan firmly on the work surface and sprinkle the almonds over the top followed by a generous sifting of confectioners' sugar. Bake for 40–45 minutes or until the cake has shrunk slightly from the sides of the pan. Run a knife around the sides of the cake, then unmold it onto a wire rack to cool. Eat on the day of baking.

$\mathscr{C}hocolate\ Cake$

──── GATEAU NOIR ────

SERVES 8

3½ oz bittersweet chocolate, chopped	*Filling*
	1½ oz candied orange peel, soaked
2 tbsp heavy cream	in 1½ tbsp each orange liqueur and
4 tbsp unsalted butter, softened and	Cognac for 4 hours
chopped	⅔ cup heavy cream
3 eggs, separated	5 oz bittersweet chocolate, chopped
5 tbsp sugar	*Icing*
6 tbsp cake flour	4 oz bittersweet chocolate, chopped
2 tbsp potato flour	4 tbsp unsalted butter, diced
small pinch of salt	chocolate leaves, to decorate

Butter a deep 8 inch cake pan. Line the bottom with buttered parchment paper, sprinkle flour over the sides and bottom and shake out excess flour. Preheat the oven to 350°F.

Melt the chocolate with the cream in a bowl placed over a saucepan of hot water. Remove from the heat, add the butter and stir gently until smooth.

Beat the egg yolks and 4 tbsp of the sugar together until thick and light and the mixture will support a trail when the beater is lifted from it. Beat the egg whites until soft peaks are formed. Sprinkle the remaining sugar over and beat again until stiff peaks are formed.

Gently fold the chocolate into the egg yolk mixture using a large metal spoon. Gently fold about one-third of the egg whites into the chocolate mixture until partially blended. Sift one-quarter of the flours and salt over, then fold in gently. Continue in this manner until all the ingredients are just evenly blended.

Spoon the mixture into the cake pan. Bake for 25–30 minutes or until well risen and just set in the center. Leave the cake to stand for a minute or so, then unmold it onto a wire rack. Remove the lining paper and leave the cake to cool.

For the filling, drain the orange peel, reserving the liquid. Bring the cream to a boil, remove from the heat and stir in the reserved liquid followed by the chocolate. Beat until smooth, then continue to beat until cooled. Stir in the candied orange peel.

Using a large serrated knife, slice the cake into 3 layers. Invert what was the top of the cake onto a serving plate and spread with half of the filling. Place the middle layer on top, spread with the remaining filling and cover with what had been the bottom layer of the cake.

For the icing, melt the chocolate in a bowl placed over a saucepan of hot water. Remove from the heat and gradually stir in the butter. Continue to stir until cooled to a spreading consistency. Spread the icing over the top and around the sides of the cake using a palette knife. Decorate with chocolate leaves.

ℐrmagnac Sponge Cake

———— GATEAU A L'ARMAGNAC ————

*C*hoose a large plate with a lip or raised edge so the cake will fit comfortably in the center.

SERVES 6

2 eggs, separated	*Syrup*
½ cup sugar	finely grated zest of 1 orange
1 cup cake flour	3 tbsp sugar
1 tsp baking powder	½ cup water
pinch of salt	4 tbsp Armagnac
2 tbsp unsalted butter, just melted	

Butter a savarin mold. Preheat the oven to 350°F.

For the syrup, gently heat the orange zest, sugar and water, stirring until the sugar has dissolved, then bring to a boil and boil, without stirring, for a couple of minutes. Remove from the heat, cover and keep warm until the cake is nearly cooked.

Beat the egg yolks and sugar together until thick and pale and the mixture will support a trail when the beater is lifted from it. Sift the flour, baking powder and salt over the surface in two or three batches, lightly folding in each batch and adding the butter with the last batch. Beat the egg whites until soft peaks are formed and fold into the mixture.

Pour into the savarin mold and bake for 20–25 minutes or until risen and springy to the touch.

Strain the syrup and add the Armagnac.

Leave the cake to stand for a minute or two before unmolding onto a large, warm plate. Slowly spoon the syrup over the top of the cake, allowing it to soak in. Leave in a cool place overnight.

Walnut Cake from Grenoble

──── GATEAU DE GRENOBLE ────

The walnuts from Grenoble, carrying an Appellation d'Origine Contrôlée, are famed throughout the world. The AOC is a legally-backed guarantee covering specific conditions relating to area of growth, the harvesting and physical characteristics.

SERVES 6–8

3 large eggs, separated
½ cup vanilla sugar
4 tbsp unsalted butter, just melted
1⅓ cups ground walnuts
1 tbsp cold, strong black coffee
1 tbsp fine bread crumbs

Butter a 7 inch springform ring mold. Preheat the oven to 350°F.

Beat the egg yolks with the sugar until pale and thick enough to support the weight of a trail of the mixture when the beater is lifted. Sprinkle the butter, nuts, coffee and bread crumbs over the surface, then, using a large metal spoon, fold them in very lightly until just evenly blended. Beat the egg whites until soft peaks are formed, and lightly fold into the walnut mixture until just blended. Spoon into the ring mold.

Bake for about 35 minutes. Leave the cake to cool for 1–2 minutes, then run the point of a sharp knife around the sides of the cake. Loosen the mold and unmold the cake onto a wire rack. Leave to cool completely.

$\mathscr{I}$ced Grape Cake

GATEAU ST VINCENT

*T*his gâteau is named in honor of the patron saint of wine – St Vincent – for not only are grapes used for the decoration and filling, but the marc or Cognac used to flavor the layers is derived from grapes. With its clear lines and glossy simplicity this is a very elegant-looking cake. For the decoration, try to use some grapes that are joined together in pairs or small bunches.

SERVES 6–8

1 quantity Whisked Sponge Cake batter (page 124)	*Filling and decoration*
	¾ cup sugar
1 quantity Fondant (page 119)	½ cup water
	5 tbsp marc or Cognac
	2 oz seedless green grapes, for glazing
	¾ lb seedless Muscat or other well-flavored green grapes, peeled

Butter a deep 8 inch cake pan, then line the bottom with buttered parchment paper. Sprinkle flour over the sides and bottom and shake out excess flour. Preheat the oven to 350°F.

Put the cake batter into the pan and bake for 10–20 minutes. Allow to cool slightly before unmolding and leaving to cool on a wire rack. When cold, cut into three layers using a large serrated knife.

For the decoration, gently heat the sugar and water in a heavy-bottomed saucepan, stirring until the sugar has dissolved. Using a pastry brush that has been dipped in hot water, brush down any sugar crystals that have formed on the side of the pan, then boil the syrup, without stirring, until the temperature reaches about 225°F on a sugar thermometer.

Pour off half of the syrup into a bowl and leave to cool slightly, then stir in the marc or Cognac. Brush the cut surfaces of the cake and the top liberally with the warm marc- or Cognac-flavored syrup, then reform the cake lightly and brush the outside liberally with the syrup.

Boil the syrup remaining in the saucepan until the temperature reaches 300°F. Dip the bottom of the saucepan immediately into cold water to stop the syrup cooking. Dip the unpeeled grapes in the syrup to coat them, allowing excess syrup to drain back into the saucepan, then leave the grapes on a wire rack for the coating to set.

Carefully separate the layers of the cake. Divide the peeled grapes in half and spread out between the layers, then reform the cake.

Gently heat the fondant in a bowl placed over a saucepan of hot water until it just feels warm. Spread the fondant evenly and smoothly over the cake. Decorate with the glazed unpeeled grapes.

Shell-Shaped Sponge Cakes

———— MADELEINES ————

There are many variations of these small, plain cakes, immortalized by Marcel Proust in his novel "A la Recherche du Temps Perdu" and strongly associated with the town of Commercy. To be worthy of any claims to being traditional they must be baked in the distinctive shell-shaped molds. Follow Proust's example and enjoy them with tilleul (lime tea) or ordinary tea or coffee, or serve with fruit or creamy desserts.

MAKES 12

2 eggs
¼ cup sugar
6 tbsp cake flour
2 tbsp potato flour or cornstarch
pinch of salt
4 tbsp unsalted butter, just melted
finely grated zest of ½ lemon

Preheat the oven to 375°F. Butter 12 madeleine molds.

Beat the eggs and sugar together until thick and pale and the mixture leaves a trail on the surface when the beater is lifted from it. Sift the flour, potato flour or cornstarch and salt together over the surface of the egg mixture in two or three batches, folding each batch in before sifting over the next. Add the butter and lemon zest with the last batch.

Spoon the mixture into the molds and bake for about 10 minutes or until golden brown. Remove the Madeleines from the molds and leave to cool on a wire rack.

$\mathscr{P}$*ine Nut Cream Cheese Cake*

—————— GATEAU AUX PIGNONS ——————

R*aspberries, wild strawberries or small or sliced strawberries, or sprigs of red currants used as a decoration will add a final touch of elegance to this luxurious yet simple cake.*

SERVES 8

4 tbsp unsalted butter, softened
1 cup vanilla sugar
2 tbsp acacia honey
1 lb cream cheese
5 eggs, separated
½ cup light cream
6 tbsp all-purpose flour
1¼ cups pine nuts, chopped
vanilla confectioners' sugar, to dredge
raspberries, sprigs of red currants, wild strawberries or
small strawberries, to decorate

Butter an 8–9 inch springform cake pan or other loose-bottomed cake pan. Preheat the oven to 325°F.

Beat the butter and sugar together until light and airy, then beat in the honey followed by the cream cheese and egg yolks and lastly the cream. Fold in the flour. Beat the egg whites until stiff peaks are formed, but not until dry, and lightly fold into the cheese mixture with the nuts.

Turn into the cake pan and bake for about 1 hour. Leave the cake to cool in the oven with the heat turned off (this will prevent the cake cracking as it cools).

Sift confectioners' sugar generously over the top and decorate with raspberries, sprigs of red currants or wild strawberries or small strawberries.

Orange Cake

──────── GATEAU A L'ORANGE ────────

SERVES 6–8

5 oranges
6 tbsp sugar
1 quantity Genoese Sponge Cake batter (page 124)
⅔ cup heavy cream
1 quantity Crème Pâtissière (page 116)
2 tbsp orange liqueur
1 quantity Rich Buttercream (page 118)
candied orange slices, to decorate

Flute one of the oranges: cut away thin parallel strips of the peel from top to bottom, using a canelle knife, and leaving strips of peel intact between the removed lines. Cut the orange across into thin slices. Remove any seeds, then lay the slices in a large skillet. Just cover with water and poach for about 20 minutes or until tender. Remove the orange slices with a slotted spoon and leave to drain on a wire rack.

Meanwhile, working over a bowl to catch the juice, peel the remaining oranges, removing all the rind and pith. Cut out the segments by slicing down between the membrane and the flesh. Add the orange juice from the bowl to the skillet, stir in the sugar and heat gently, stirring, until it has dissolved. Carefully add the orange segments and poach for 3–5 minutes. Transfer the segments to the wire rack using a slotted spoon. Boil the liquid until reduced to a thick, syrupy glaze, adding any juices that come from the slices and segments.

Place the orange segments on a tray that they just fit, pour the syrup over and leave to cool.

Butter a deep 8 inch round cake pan, then line the bottom with buttered parchment paper. Preheat the oven to 375°F.

Put the cake batter into the prepared pan and bake for 25–30 minutes or until springy to the touch and the sides have shrunk slightly from the sides of the pan. Leave to stand for 1–2 minutes before unmolding onto a wire rack to cool.

Whip the cream until peaks are formed, then lightly fold into the crème pâtissière.

Beat half of the orange liqueur into the buttercream.

Carefully cut the cake into three layers using a large, serrated knife.

Lift the orange segments from the syrup using a slotted spoon, allowing the excess syrup to drain off. Add the remaining liqueur to the syrup and brush the cut surfaces of the cake with the syrup. Place the bottom cake layer on a serving plate and spread with half of the crème pâtissière. Place half of the orange segments on top. Cover with another layer of sponge, then the rest of the crème pâtissière and orange segments. Finish with the top layer of sponge. Coat the top and sides of the cake with some of the buttercream and spoon the remainder into a pastry bag fitted with a small star tube. Decorate the cake with piped buttercream, the poached orange slices, and the candied orange slices.

$\mathcal{F}$resh Fig Slices

—————— PETITES TRANCHES AUX FIGUES ——————

A very simple, light "biscuit" mixture is used in the making of these delicate pastries. It is not possible to make this quantity of crème pâtissière accurately, so you will have to reserve some from a batch made for another purpose.

SERVES 4

½ cup + 2 tbsp cake flour
2 egg whites
¾ cup confectioners' sugar, sifted
5 tbsp unsalted butter, just melted
⅓ cup Crème Pâtissière (page 116)
1 oz almond paste (page 9)
1½ tbsp Kirsch
⅔ cup heavy cream
about 8 large ripe figs, depending on size, peeled if necessary and thinly sliced
vanilla confectioners' sugar, to dredge

Preheat the oven to 350°F. Mark 12 rectangles, each 3½ × 1½ inches, on buttered baking sheets.

Mix the flour, egg whites and confectioners' sugar together, then stir in the butter to make a smooth thick batter. Spread the mixture evenly in the marked rectangles and bake for about 10 minutes or until golden. Quickly remove the rectangles from the baking sheets using a palette knife and leave to cool on a wire rack.

Mix the crème pâtissière with the almond paste and Kirsch in a blender, then pour into a bowl. Whip the cream until it stands in soft peaks and lightly fold it into the mixture.

Reserve a few slices of fig for decoration, and divide the remaining slices into two equal portions.

Spread the crème pâtissière mixture over one-third of the rectangles and cover with one portion of the fig slices. Place another rectangle on top of each and repeat the layering, ending up with a final rectangle. Sift confectioners' sugar liberally over the surface and mark lines with a very hot skewer, if liked. Decorate with the reserved slices of fig.

Illustrated on page 90

$\mathscr{H}$azelnut and Red Currant Cake

——— GATEAU AUX NOISETTES ET GROSEILLES ———

SERVES 6–8

2 eggs
⅔ cup sugar
½ cup cake flour
½ cup coarsely ground, lightly toasted hazelnuts (filberts)
6 tbsp water
1 pint red currants
2 tsp arrowroot
1 tbsp lemon juice
1 tbsp eau-de-vie de groseille or de framboise (optional)
⅔ cup crème fraîche or heavy cream
¼ cup fromage blanc or frais
confectioners' sugar, to decorate

Butter an 8 inch layer cake pan, then dust with flour and shake out the excess. Finally, dust with sugar. Preheat the oven to 350°F.

Beat the eggs and 6 tbsp of the sugar together until very light and thick enough to support a trail of mixture on the surface. Sift the flour over the surface and fold in very gently with the ground hazelnuts using a metal spoon. Spoon into the cake pan and level the surface.

Bake for about 25 minutes or until well risen and lightly browned. Leave to cool in the pan for 10 minutes, then carefully transfer to a wire rack to cool completely.

Meanwhile, gently heat the remaining sugar and water in a small saucepan, stirring until the sugar has dissolved. Reserve a few of the red currants for decoration and add the remainder to the sugar syrup. Cook gently, shaking the pan occasionally, until the fruit has softened.

Blend the arrowroot to a smooth paste with a little water. Gently stir into the fruit and bring to a boil, stirring gently. Simmer for about 1 minute or until the liquid clears and thickens. Remove from the heat and stir in the lemon juice and eau-de-vie or an equal amount of extra water. Leave to cool, then cover and chill.

To complete the gâteau, cut the cake into two equal layers. Whip the crème fraîche or cream with the fromage blanc or frais until soft peaks form. Spread over the cut surface of the bottom layer, cover with the red currant mixture and place the top layer on top, pressing down lightly. Sift confectioners' sugar over the top and decorate with whipped cream and the reserved red currants.

Illustrated on page 91

Fresh Fig Slices

Hazelnut and Red Currant Cake

Cookies

Orange Cookies

─── PALAIS DES DAMES ───

*T*hese crisp cookies, which may also be spelled Palets des Dames, are a "classic" petit four. They
* may be flavored with lemon zest instead of orange, and the crystallized orange peel can be
replaced by currants or golden raisins soaked in Cognac or rum. The cookies may also be coated
with thin glacé icing. Orange sugar is made by leaving a long strip of orange zest in a jar of sugar.

MAKES ABOUT 24

3 tbsp finely chopped crystallized orange peel
1 tbsp orange liqueur
7 tbsp unsalted butter, softened
½ cup orange sugar
2 egg whites, lightly beaten with a fork
⅔ cup all-purpose flour
small pinch of salt

Leave the orange peel to steep in the liqueur for 1 hour, then drain and pat dry. Preheat the oven to
400°F. Line two baking sheets with parchment paper.

Using a wooden spoon, beat the butter, add the sugar and beat until the mixture is light and fluffy.
Gradually beat in the egg whites, beating well after each addition. Sift the flour and salt over the mixture
and lightly fold it in using a metal spoon.

Spoon the mixture into a pastry bag fitted with a ½ inch plain tube and pipe in 1 inch wide mounds on the
baking sheets, leaving plenty of room between them to allow them to spread. Sprinkle the orange peel over
the surface. Bake for 8–10 minutes or until the cookies are golden brown around the edges.

Carefully transfer the cookies to a wire rack to cool.

Illustrated on page 98

$\mathcal{I}$ced Almond Shortbread

SABLES NANTAIS

MAKES ABOUT 24

1 cup all-purpose flour	*Icing*
pinch of salt	½ cup confectioners' sugar
¼ tsp baking powder	2 tsp Kirsch
10 tbsp unsalted butter, chopped	2 tsp cold water
¼ cup sugar	
⅔ cup freshly ground almonds	
1½ tsp Cognac	
⅓ cup sliced almonds	

Preheat the oven to 350°F.

Sift the flour, salt and baking powder into a bowl. Toss in the butter, then cut it in until the mixture resembles bread crumbs. Stir in the sugar and ground almonds and sprinkle the Cognac over the surface. Using one hand, form the mixture into a ball. Cover and chill for 3–4 hours.

Leave the dough at room temperature for a few minutes to soften slightly, then roll it out on a lightly floured surface, using a lightly floured rolling pin, to ⅛ inch thick. Using a lightly floured 2 inch cutter, cut the dough into rounds. Carefully transfer to buttered baking sheets, leaving about ½ inch between them, and scatter the sliced almonds over the tops. Bake for about 15 minutes or until light golden.

Leave the cookies to stand for 1–2 minutes before transferring to a wire rack to cool.

For the icing, sift the confectioners' sugar into a bowl, add the Kirsch and water and beat until smooth. The icing should coat the back of the spoon, so if necessary, add another 1 tsp cold water.

Using a spoon, pour small amounts of the icing over the tops of the cookies. Leave to set.

Illustrated on page 99

Cornets with Bilberries and Cream

—————— CORNETS AUX MYRTILLES ——————

Like Cigarettes Russes and Tuiles d'Amandes, the cornets have to be baked and shaped in batches. They can be kept for a few days in an airtight container, but they are fragile so handle and store them with care. Bilberries are one of the popular fruits in Alsace, from where this recipe comes, but if you cannot get any, other soft fruits such as raspberries, red currants or sliced strawberries can be used instead.

MAKES ABOUT 12

2 egg whites	*Filling*
5 tbsp superfine sugar	⅔ cup heavy cream
6 tbsp all-purpose flour	sifted confectioners' sugar, to taste
pinch of salt	2 cups bilberries or small
4 tbsp unsalted butter, melted and cooled	blackberries

Preheat the oven to 400°F. Butter two or more large baking sheets.

Beat the egg whites until frothy, then add the sugar and beat for 2–3 minutes or until thick. Sift the flour and salt over the top of the mixture in two or three batches, folding it in lightly with a metal spoon between each batch and adding the butter with the last batch. Place spoonfuls of the mixture well apart on the baking sheets and spread them out to rounds about 3–3½ inches in diameter. Bake for 5–6 minutes or until the edges are a pale golden brown.

Immediately after they are taken from the oven, carefully remove the cookies individually from the baking sheet and wrap them around oiled cornucopia molds. Leave to cool and set on a wire rack, then carefully slip out the molds.

Just before serving, whip the cream until it begins to thicken. Sprinkle a little confectioners' sugar over and continue to whip until it stands in soft peaks. Reserve a little of the cream and mix the remainder with most of the fruit. Use this mixture to fill the cornets. Spoon the reserved cream into a pastry bag fitted with a small star tube and decorate the cornets together with the reserved fruit.

Aniseed Cookies

———— GALETTES D'ANIS DE FLAVIGNY ————

MAKES ABOUT 18

6 tbsp sugar
1 cup freshly ground almonds
scant ½ tsp ground aniseed
1 egg white
about ½ cup pine nuts, chopped

Preheat the oven to 325°F. Butter a baking sheet, sprinkle flour over it and shake off the excess.

Pound the sugar and almonds together in a mortar, then pass through a sieve. Stir in the aniseed. Lightly break up the egg white with a fork. Bind the almond mixture together with the egg white until smooth.

Break off small pieces and roll them into small balls. Flatten the balls slightly, press a few pieces of pine nut on top and place on the baking sheet. Bake for about 45 minutes or until dry.

Transfer to a wire rack to cool.

Cream Cookies

———— GALETTE NORMANDE ————

MAKES 8

¾ cup all-purpose flour
pinch of salt
½ cup vanilla sugar
½ cup heavy cream
1 egg, lightly beaten with 1 tsp water, to glaze

Preheat the oven to 350°F. Then butter a 7 inch tart ring and place it on a buttered baking sheet or use a tart pan with a removable base.

Sift the flour and salt into a bowl. Stir in the sugar. Using a round-bladed knife, stir in the cream, and quickly and lightly form the mixture into a dough. Knead briefly, then form a round to fit inside the tart ring. Brush the top with the egg glaze and bake for 30–40 minutes.

Mark the surface into eight triangular wedges and leave to cool slightly, then carefully transfer to a wire rack to cool completely.

Crisp Rolled Cookies

──────── CIGARETTES RUSSES ────────

You will need at least two baking sheets and several wooden spoons plus a reasonable amount of time to make these crisp cookies because it is only possible to bake a few at a time, and they must be rolled as soon as they come out of the oven. Should any harden before you have been able to curl them, put them back in the oven for a minute to soften up.

MAKES ABOUT 18

2 egg whites
1 cup vanilla confectioners' sugar, sifted
5 tbsp all-purpose flour, sifted
small pinch of salt
5 tbsp unsalted butter, melted

Preheat the oven to 400°F. Butter at least two large baking sheets, sprinkle flour over them and shake off the excess.

Beat the egg whites until stiff, then gradually beat in the sugar followed by the flour and salt. Beat in the melted butter. Drop 2 or 3 spoonfuls of the mixture on the baking sheets, leaving plenty of room between them, and spread out each spoonful with a wet knife. Bake for 5–6 minutes or until golden brown.

Immediately after they are taken from the oven, remove them individually from the baking sheet and wrap them around the handle of an oiled wooden spoon. Leave to cool and harden on a wire rack then carefully slip off the wooden spoon. Repeat until all the mixture has been used up.

Illustrated on page 102

Orange Cookies

Iced Almond Shortbread

Almond Wafers

TUILES D'AMANDES

Tuiles d'Amandes are so called because their shape resembles that of traditional Provençal roof tiles. They can be kept in an airtight container for several days.

MAKES ABOUT 20

2 egg whites
½ cup + 2 tbsp vanilla confectioners' sugar
7 tbsp all-purpose flour, sifted
small pinch of salt
⅔ cup ground almonds
4 tbsp unsalted butter, heated until pourable but not melted
few drops of almond extract
½ cup sliced almonds

Preheat the oven to 425°F. Lightly butter two or three large baking sheets.

Beat the egg whites and sugar with a fork until frothy, then add the flour, salt and ground almonds. Mix in the butter with the almond extract. Drop spoonfuls of the mixture onto the baking sheets, leaving plenty of room between them to allow for spreading and adjusting the size according to the size of the tuile required. Using a damp knife, spread out each spoonful to a thin flat round. Sprinkle sliced almonds over each one.

Bake for 5–7 minutes or until golden and lightly tinged with brown around the edges. Immediately after they are taken from the oven, remove the cookies from the baking sheet with a palette knife and drape them over a rolling pin or oiled bottle, with the almonds outermost. If the cookies begin to harden before they are removed from the baking sheet, put them back in the oven for a few moments to soften. Leave the tuiles to cool and harden into shape, then carefully transfer them to a wire rack to cool completely. Continue to cook in batches until all the mixture has been used.

Illustrated on page 102

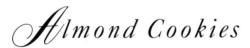 *A*lmond Cookies

MACAROONS

*M*acaroons have been made in Lorraine for eight centuries or more. By the end of the seventeenth century, those made in Nancy, by the nuns of the convent, had already established a good reputation, and when they were evicted from their convent during the French Revolution, the sisters started a bakery (which still exists in the rue des Soeurs) producing macaroons to earn a livelihood. The high reputation of Nancy macaroons still exists. Nuns and monks in other places, such as Melun and Cormery, also made macaroons and today they are also ones to look out for. Macaroons should be light, crisp on the outside yet soft and moist in the center, and not too sweet. To enjoy macaroons at their best eat them while they are fresh, but they will keep for 1–2 weeks if stored in an airtight container.

MAKES ABOUT 12

1½–2 egg whites
1⅓ cups freshly ground almonds
⅔ cup vanilla sugar
about 6 blanched almonds, split (optional)
confectioners' sugar, to dredge

Preheat the oven to 400°F. Line a heavy baking sheet with parchment paper.

In a mortar, using a pestle, gradually work ½ egg white into the ground almonds until a smooth, fine paste is formed. Work in half of the sugar, then add another ½ egg white in the same way. Follow by the remaining sugar and another ½ egg white to make a mixture that is soft but not runny. If the mixture is too stiff, work in a little more egg white.

Divide the mixture into about 12 portions and roll in your hands to make walnut-sized balls. Place them on the baking sheet and flatten them slightly. Lightly press a split almond on top, if used. Brush lightly with a little water, then sift confectioners' sugar over the surface. Bake for 18–20 minutes or until lightly browned.

Pour a glass of cold water between the lining paper and the baking sheet – the steam this creates makes it easier to remove the macaroons. Leave for a few minutes, then carefully lift the macaroons from the lining paper and leave on a wire rack to cool.

Illustrated on page 103

Almond Wafers & Crisp Rolled Cookies

Almond Cookies

Yeast Breads & Cakes

Walnut and Raisin Bread

PAIN DE NOIX ET RAISINS

This bread can be served while it is still warm or at room temperature.

MAKES 1 LOAF

½ oz compressed yeast, or 1 package active dry yeast
½ cup lukewarm milk
1⅓ cups bread flour
½ tsp salt
scant 1 cup rye flour
¼ cup sugar
1 egg, lightly beaten
4 tbsp unsalted butter, softened and diced
1 cup chopped walnuts
¾ cup raisins
1 egg, lightly beaten with 1 tsp water, to glaze

Cream the compressed yeast with the milk, or stir the dry yeast into the milk until dissolved, then leave in a warm place until frothy, about 20 minutes.

Sift the bread flour and salt into the bowl of a heavy duty (countertop) electric mixer. Stir in the rye flour and sugar then add the yeast mixture and egg and work into a dough using the dough hook. Work the dough until it no longer sticks to the sides of the bowl, and is smooth and elastic. If necessary add a little extra milk. Cover the bowl with a damp cloth and leave in a warm place to rise until doubled in bulk.

Butter a baking sheet.

Turn the dough onto a lightly floured surface. Punch down, then knead, work in the butter, until smooth and elastic again. Add the walnuts and raisins toward the end of the kneading. Form the dough into a loaf shape, about 3 × 8 inches, on the baking sheet. With a sharp knife, make two or three parallel diagonal slashes on the top of the loaf. Cover loosely with a damp cloth and leave in a warm place until well risen.

Preheat the oven to 350°F.

Brush the loaf with the egg glaze, then bake for about 30 minutes or until the top is browned and the loaf sounds hollow when tapped with the knuckles on the base. Transfer to a wire rack to cool.

Illustrated on page 106

$\mathscr{B}$rioche

BRIOCHE A TETE

MAKES 1 LARGE OR 9 SMALL BRIOCHES

½ oz compressed yeast, or 1 package active dry yeast
5 tbsp lukewarm milk
1¾ cups bread flour
½ tsp salt
2 tbsp sugar
3 eggs, beaten
1 stick unsalted butter, softened and chopped
1 egg yolk, lightly beaten with 1 tsp water, to glaze

Cream the compressed yeast with the milk, or stir the dry yeast into the milk until dissolved, then leave in a warm place until frothy, about 20 minutes.

Sift the flour and salt into the bowl of a heavy duty (countertop) electric mixer. Stir in the sugar and then the yeast liquid followed by the eggs. Work the ingredients using the dough hook until the dough is smooth and elastic. Cover the bowl and leave at warm room temperature until doubled in bulk, about 2 hours.

Turn the dough onto a work surface. Punch down and knead it for about 5 minutes or until smooth and elastic and small bubbles appear just beneath the surface. Work in the butter in small pieces, a few at a time, squeezing the butter between your fingers to soften it, then squeezing it into the dough. Continue until all the butter has been incorporated. Work the dough briefly until smooth, then return to the bowl, cover and chill, overnight if convenient. This will firm up the butter and make the dough more manageable.

Butter an 8–9 inch diameter brioche mold.

Turn the dough onto a lightly floured surface and knead lightly. Divide off one-quarter of the dough. Roll the larger piece into a ball and place in the brioche mold. Cut a cross in the top of the ball with the point of a sharp knife. Form the smaller piece of dough into a ball, then pull out one side slightly into a point. Nestle the small ball, pointed end downward, into the cross on the larger ball of dough. Cover and leave to rise in a warm place until doubled in bulk – about 35–45 minutes.

Preheat the oven to 400°F.

Brush the brioche lightly with the egg glaze, then bake for about 30 minutes or until risen and golden on top. Transfer to a wire rack to cool.

For *Small Brioches*, follow the recipe above, but use 9 small brioche molds. Divide the dough into nine portions. Take one-quarter off each portion (for the small topknot ball) and shape the remainder of each portion into a ball. Place in the molds and snip the top of each ball with scissors to make a cross. Form the reserved small portions of dough into balls, pull out one side into a point, and place on top of the dough in the molds. Cover and leave in a warm place to rise until doubled in size.

Bake as for large brioche, allowing 20 minutes.

Illustrated on page 11

Walnut and Raisin Bread

Almond & Plain Croissants

$\mathscr{C}$roissants

―――――――――――――― CROISSANTS ――――――――――――――

*I*n France, where croissants are synonymous with breakfast, no one would think of making their
*own, but in this country sources of good croissants are limited, and even where they do
exist may not be open early enough. So if you want good croissants you have to make them yourself.
It is not necessary to stay up most of the night making them. They can be prepared up to the baking
stage and then left, covered, in the refrigerator overnight. Leave them at room temperature for
30 minutes before baking.*

MAKES 8

½ oz compressed yeast, or 1 package active dry yeast
⅔ cup lukewarm milk
1⅔ cups bread flour
1 tsp salt
1 tsp sugar
1 egg yolk, beaten
1 stick unsalted butter, diced and chilled
1 egg yolk, lightly beaten with 1 tsp water, to glaze

Cream the compressed yeast with the milk, or stir the dry yeast into the milk until dissolved, then leave in a warm place until frothy, about 20 minutes.

Sift the flour and salt into the bowl of a heavy duty (countertop) electric mixer. Stir in the sugar and then the yeast mixture and egg yolk. Work into a dough using the dough hook. Work the dough until it becomes smooth and elastic.

Cover the bowl with a damp cloth and leave the dough in a warm place to rise until doubled in bulk, about 1½ hours.

Turn the dough onto a lightly floured surface. Punch down, then roll out to a large rectangle about 12 × 6 inches. Dot about one-third of the butter over the bottom two-thirds of the dough, leaving a border of about ½ inch clear around the sides. Fold the top third of the dough down over the butter and the bottom third up over it. Press the edges together with the rolling pin to seal them. Turn the dough through 45° (make a faint thumb mark in the dough to show which way around it was on the surface – i.e. on either the right or left side, and remember which it was!). Place on an oiled plate, cover and chill for 30 minutes.

Return the dough to the work surface in the same position that it was. Repeat the rolling out, dotting with butter, folding and chilling until all the butter has been used. Repeat the rolling, folding and chilling process once more.

Butter one large or two small baking sheets.

Roll out the dough on a lightly floured surface, using a lightly floured rolling pin, to a 12–14 inch square that is under ¼ inch thick. Using a sharp knife, trim the edges, then cut the large square into four small that is under ¼ inch thick. Using a sharp knife, trim the edges, then cut the large square into four small squares and each small square into two triangles.

Brush the two shorter sides of each triangle lightly with egg glaze, then lightly roll up from the long side toward the point. Place on the baking sheet with the point underneath and curl the two ends in to form a crescent shape. Cover and leave in a warm place to rise until doubled in bulk.

Preheat the oven to 425°F.

Brush the croissants with egg glaze then bake for 15–20 minutes or until golden brown. If the croissants are on two baking sheets, bake them separately. Serve warm.

Illustrated on page 107

Almond Croissants

CROISSANTS D'AMANDES

MAKES 8

1 quantity risen Croissant dough (page 108)
¼ lb almond paste (page 9)
1 egg, lightly beaten with 1 tsp water, to glaze
1 cup sliced almonds
confectioners' sugar, to dredge

Butter one large or two smaller baking sheets.

Cut the dough into eight triangles, following the instructions above. Divide the almond paste into eight pieces and roll each piece into a cigar-shape. Place a piece of almond paste near the long side of each dough triangle. Brush the two shorter sides of each triangle lightly with egg glaze, then roll up from the long side toward the point. Place the croissants on the baking sheet, point underneath and curl the two ends in to form a crescent.

Cover and leave to rise in a warm place until doubled in bulk.

Preheat the oven to 400°F. Brush the tops of the croissants with egg glaze and sprinkle with sliced almonds. Bake for about 20 minutes.

Transfer to a wire rack, sift confectioners' sugar over and serve while still warm.

Illustrated on page 107

Yeast Cake with Crystallized Fruits

———— GATEAU GOUBAUD ————

The various recipes that I have found for this enriched bread go no further than to say that the fruits should be crystallized. I suggest a mixture of pineapple, apricots, citron and stem ginger. The mixture is probably not traditional, and is rather extravagant, but it does seem appropriate for what is hardly an everyday loaf. Whatever blend of fruits you choose, I strongly recommend including the ginger as it is an interesting contrast to the dough.

SERVES 8

½ lb crystallized fruits, chopped (about 1⅓ cups)	*Icing*
	½ cup confectioners' sugar, sifted
4 tbsp orange liqueur	lemon juice or water
1 quantity risen Brioche dough (page 105), chilled overnight	

Soak the fruits in the liqueur for about 1 hour, then remove with a slotted spoon. Reserve any remaining liquid.

Butter an 8 inch springform cake pan.

Punch down the dough, then divide it in half. Roll out one piece to a round 8 inches in diameter and place in the bottom of the pan. Divide the other piece of dough into 13 equal portions.

Roll out 12 of the pieces to rough diamond shapes. Divide most of the fruits between them, placing the fruit in the center of the widest part of the diamond. Fold the dough lengthwise over the fruit and seal the joins together as securely as possible. Pack these pieces into the pan so they are pointing inward.

Roll out the remaining piece of dough into a round. Place the remaining fruit in the center and fold the dough over it to form into a round bun shape. Use this to fill the center of the pan.

Cover and leave in a warm place to rise until doubled in size.

Preheat the oven to 400°F.

Bake the cake for about 25 minutes or until browned. Meanwhile, blend the confectioners' sugar with sufficient lemon juice or water to make an icing that coats the back of a spoon.

Carefully remove the cake from the pan and put it, right way up, on a wire rack. Brush the top of the cake with any remaining liqueur, then spoon the icing over. Serve warm.

$\mathscr{R}$um Babas

—————— BABAS AU RHUM ——————

$\mathscr{T}$raditional rum babas, made from a savarin dough, are baked in tall, plain molds that are slightly wider at the rim than the base.

MAKES 8

½ oz compressed yeast, or 1 package active dry yeast	*Syrup*
6 tbsp lukewarm milk	⅔ cup sugar
1⅔ cups bread flour	1¼ cups water
1 tsp salt	strip of lemon zest
2 tsp sugar	5 tbsp rum
4 eggs, beaten	
1 stick unsalted butter, softened	
⅔ cup golden raisins	
Apricot Glaze (page 9), warmed	

Cream the compressed yeast with the milk, or stir the dry yeast into the milk until dissolved, then leave in a warm place until frothy, about 20 minutes.

Sift the flour and salt into the bowl of a heavy duty (countertop) electric mixer. Stir in the sugar followed by the yeast mixture. Beat in the eggs and, using the dough hook, work until smooth and elastic.

Cover the bowl with a cloth and leave in a warm place to rise until doubled in bulk, about 1½ hours. Butter 8 baba or dariole molds of 5 fl oz capacity.

Punch down the dough. Gradually beat the butter into the dough until the dough is smooth. Knead in the raisins, incorporating them evenly. Divide the dough between the molds so that each one is about two-thirds full. Place the molds on a baking sheet, cover loosely and leave in a warm place to rise until the dough fills the molds.

Preheat the oven to 350°F. Bake the babas for about 15 minutes or until golden brown. Allow to cool for about 5 minutes before transferring to a wire rack to cool to lukewarm.

For the syrup, gently heat the sugar and water in a heavy-bottomed saucepan, stirring until the sugar has dissolved. Add the lemon zest, then bring to a boil and boil, without stirring, for 5 minutes. Remove from the heat and cool slightly, then add 4 tbsp of the rum.

Place the babas in a dish. Prick them all over, then slowly spoon the warm syrup over, letting as much as possible be absorbed. Leave the babas to soak for several hours, spooning any syrup that seeps from the babas back over them.

Add the remaining rum to the warm apricot glaze and brush over the babas before serving.

Illustrated on page 10

Rich Yeast Cake with Raisins

KUGELHOPF

SERVES 8

½ cup raisins
½ oz compressed yeast, or 1 package active dry yeast
½ cup lukewarm milk
1⅔ cups bread flour
½ tsp salt
2 tbsp vanilla sugar
2 eggs, beaten
2 tbsp rum
2½ tbsp chopped mixed candied peel
2 tsp finely grated orange zest
2 tsp finely grated lemon zest
⅓ cup slivered almonds
6 tbsp unsalted butter, softened and diced
confectioners' sugar, to dredge

Pour boiling water over the raisins and leave to soak.

Cream the compressed yeast with the milk, or stir the dry yeast into the milk until dissolved, then leave in a warm place until frothy, about 20 minutes.

Sift the flour and salt into the bowl of a heavy duty (countertop) electric mixer. Stir in the sugar and make a well in the center. Pour the eggs, rum and yeast liquid into the well. Using the dough hook, work into a smooth dough. Work the dough until it is firm and elastic.

Cover the bowl with a damp cloth and leave in a warm place to rise until doubled in bulk.

Drain the raisins well, then mix with the peel and fruit zest. Butter an 8 inch kugelhopf pan and sprinkle the almonds over the inside.

Turn the dough onto a lightly floured work surface. Punch down and knead it for about 5 minutes or until smooth and elastic. Work in the butter in small pieces, then the fruit mixture. Work the dough briefly to incorporate the ingredients evenly.

Place the dough in the pan, cover with a damp cloth and leave in a warm place until well risen, about 30–40 minutes.

Preheat the oven to 400°F.

Place the pan in the oven, then reduce the temperature to 350°F and bake the kugelhopf for 35–40 minutes or until the top is browned and the sides shrunk from the pan.

Leave to cool for 2–3 minutes, then transfer to a wire rack to cool completely. Sift confectioners' sugar over the surface just before serving.

Chocolate-Filled Brioches

—————— PETITS PAINS AU CHOCOLAT ——————

*I*n France, these are sold fresh from the oven in the afternoon to revive children after school, as well as in the morning alongside croissants and brioches. They are well worth making to be enjoyed at any time of day, and it is quite permissible to dunk pains au chocolat in your coffee, if that is how you like to eat them. Coffee-dunked or not, these must be eaten while still warm from the oven.

MAKES 12–14

1 quantity risen Brioche dough (page 105), chilled overnight
about 4 oz thin block semisweet chocolate
1 egg, lightly beaten with 1 tsp water, to glaze

Butter a baking sheet.

Place a long-bladed sharp knife in very hot water for a few minutes then, exerting as little pressure as possible, cut the chocolate into 12–14 strips, reheating the knife frequently.

Divide the dough into 12–14 pieces and shape each piece into a rectangle large enough to enclose a piece of chocolate completely. Brush the edges of the dough with the egg glaze, place the chocolate on top and fold over. Press the edges together to seal them. Place the brioches on the baking sheet, cover and leave in a warm place to rise until doubled in bulk.

Preheat the oven to 400°F. Brush the brioches with egg glaze and place in the oven. Reduce the temperature to 375°F and bake for 12–15 minutes or until golden brown on the outside and the chocolate is just beginning to melt inside.

Transfer to a wire rack to cool slightly.

 pice Bread

—— PAIN D'EPICES ——

Pains d'épices are made in many areas of France. The sometimes-seen translation of the name as "gingerbread" can be misleading because some pains d'épices are based on a yeast dough. Also, different spices are frequently included, such as the anise which is almost always used in Burgundy, and they contain rye flour which tends to make a loaf that is on the heavy side and a little dry – quite unlike our moist gingerbreads.

MAKES 2 LOAVES

1¾ oz compressed yeast, or 3 packages active dry yeast
1½ cups lukewarm water
3¼ cups rye flour
2⅓ cups bread flour
2½ tsp ground ginger
2½ tsp ground allspice
pinch of salt
1½ tbsp whole aniseed
2½ tbsp brown sugar
¼ cup clear honey
4 tbsp unsalted butter, softened
milk, to glaze
butter, to serve

Cream the compressed yeast with the warm water, or stir the dry yeast with the water until dissolved, then leave in a warm place until frothy, about 20 minutes.

Sift the flours, ginger, allspice and salt into the bowl of a heavy duty (countertop) mixer. Stir in the aniseed and sugar and make a well in the center. Add the yeast mixture and work into a dough using the dough hook. Continue to work the dough until it becomes smooth and elastic.

Cover the bowl with a damp cloth and leave in a warm place to rise until doubled in bulk, about 1½ hours.

Turn the dough onto a lightly floured surface. Punch down then gradually work in the honey and the very soft butter. When evenly blended and smooth, divide the dough in half and form each piece into an oval shape. Place on a large buttered and floured baking sheet, cover with a damp cloth and leave in a warm place to rise until almost doubled in bulk, about 45 minutes to 1 hour.

Preheat the oven to 375°F.

Brush the tops of the loaves with milk, then bake for 30–35 minutes or until the loaves sound hollow when tapped on the base.

Transfer to a wire rack to cool. Serve sliced, with butter.

Basic Recipes

Pastry Cream or Confectioner's Custard

———————— CREME PATISSIERE ————————

*T*he addition of cornstarch gives this custard a translucent and glossy appearance. The vanilla bean can be rinsed, dried and used again. Crème pâtissière can be kept in a cool place for no longer than a day, or in the refrigerator for up to 2 days.

MAKES 1¼ cups

1 vanilla bean
1¼ cups milk
4 egg yolks
¼ cup sugar
3 tbsp all-purpose flour
2 tsp cornstarch
pinch of salt

Add the vanilla bean to the milk and bring to scalding point, then remove from the heat, cover and leave to infuse for 20 minutes.

Whisk the egg yolks and sugar together with a balloon whisk until thick and light and the mixture will support a trail when the whisk is lifted from it. Mix the flours and salt together and stir into the egg mixture.

Remove the vanilla bean from the milk. Heat the milk to scalding point again, then slowly pour it onto the egg mixture, whisking continuously. Rinse the saucepan, pour the custard back into it and heat gently, whisking, until it comes to the boil. Adjust the heat so the custard simmers and cook, still whisking, for 2–3 minutes. Pass through a sieve.

If the crème pâtissière is not to be used immediately, cover the surface closely with plastic wrap or dot small pieces of unsalted butter over the surface, to prevent a skin forming.

Almond Pastry Cream

—————— CREME FRANGIPANE ——————

*O*ver the course of the centuries, the name "frangipane" has been applied to a number of different products. In the sixteenth century in France, the name "frangipane" referred to a perfume for gloves made from Mexican red jasmine by the Italian Marchese Muzio Frangipani. In the eighteenth century, it became the name for pâtisserie fillings that were flavored with almond and orange flower water. Then, in the nineteenth century, the flower that gave the perfume became known as frangipani. Crème frangipane can be kept in a cool place for no longer than a day, or up to 2 days in the refrigerator.

MAKES 1¼ cups

1 vanilla bean, split
1¼ cups milk
3 egg yolks
6 tbsp sugar
¼ cup all-purpose flour
2 tsp cornstarch
3 tbsp unsalted butter
1 cup freshly ground almonds, or scant 1 cup crushed macaroons
(if these are used reduce the sugar slightly)

Add the vanilla bean to the milk and heat gently to scalding point, then remove from the heat, cover and leave to infuse for 20 minutes.

Whisk the egg yolks and sugar together until thick and light and the mixture will support a trail when the whisk is lifted from it. Mix the flour and cornstarch together and stir into the egg mixture.

Remove the vanilla bean from the milk. Heat the milk to scalding point again, then slowly pour it onto the egg mixture, whisking continuously. Rinse the saucepan, pour the custard back into it and bring to a boil, whisking gently. Adjust the heat so the mixture simmers and cook for 2–3 minutes, stirring with a wooden spoon.

Pass through a sieve, then stir in the butter and almonds or macaroons. If the crème frangipane is not to be used immediately, cover the surface closely with plastic wrap or place small pieces of unsalted butter on the surface, to prevent a skin forming.

Rich Buttercream

—————————— CREME AU BEURRE ——————————

Crème au beurre not only adds a special quality to the flavor and texture of pâtisserie, but also enhances the appearance because it holds its shape when piped. Crème au beurre can be made in advance and kept, covered, in the refrigerator, but it must be allowed to soften up at room temperature before it is used.

MAKES ½ lb

½ cup sugar
½ cup water
4 egg yolks, beaten
2 sticks (8 oz) unsalted butter, softened

Gently heat the sugar and water in a heavy-bottomed saucepan, stirring with a wooden spoon until the sugar has dissolved, then bring to a boil and boil, without stirring, until the temperature reaches 240°F on a candy thermometer.

Gradually pour the syrup onto the egg yolks, beating continuously, and continue to beat until the mixture is thick and cool.

Gradually beat in the butter until the mixture is smooth and shiny.

$\mathcal{F}$*ondant*

FONDANT

$\mathcal{T}$o use fondant, warm it gently in a bowl placed over a saucepan of hot water until it softens.

MAKES 1 lb

2 cups sugar
1 cup water
1 tsp glycerin

Sprinkle cold water over a marble slab or other suitable work suface to dampen if evenly.

Gently heat the sugar in the water in a heavy-bottomed saucepan, stirring with a wooden spoon until the sugar has dissolved. Add the glycerin. Bring to a boil and boil, without stirring, until the temperature reaches 240°F on a candy thermometer. Immediately dip the base of the saucepan in cold water, then quickly pour the syrup onto the dampened surface to form a pool.

Leave to cool for a few minutes, then, using a dampened large metal spatula, fold the sides of the pool of syrup to the center. Continue to do this until the syrup becomes glossy and viscous and has a faint yellow tinge. Then work the mixture, using a wooden spatula, in a continuous figure of eight action for 5–10 minutes until it becomes white, crumbly and difficult to work. With lightly wetted hands, form the mixture into a ball. Knead it by pushing half of the ball away from you with the heel of one hand and then fold the pushed out portion back into the ball using a metal palette knife or scraper. Continue in this fashion, in a flowing action, for 5–10 minutes or until there are no lumps and the mixture feels smooth.

Form the fondant into a neat ball, place it on a dampened plate, cover with a thick, damp cloth and leave in a cool place for at least 12 hours before using.

$\mathcal{E}$nriched Pie Pastry

PATE BRISEE

MAKES ¾ cup quantity

¾ cup all-purpose flour
small pinch of salt
5 tbsp unsalted butter, at room temperature
1 egg yolk

Sift the flour and salt onto a cold work surface and form a well in the center. Pound the butter with a rolling pin to soften it slightly, then chop it roughly with a cold knife. Put the lumps into the well with the egg yolk. Quickly and lightly blend them together by "pecking" at them with the fingertips until they are just beginning to bind and look rather like rough scrambled egg.

Sprinkle a little of the flour over the butter/egg mixture and, as lightly and quickly as possible, draw all the ingredients together by chopping through them with a cold round-bladed knife while at the same time drawing free flour from the edges of the pile into the center with a smooth, flowing action.

When there is no free fat or flour to be seen and the mixture resembles crumbs draw it lightly into a ball with the fingertips. Knead it once or twice with the heel of the hand to ensure the ingredients are evenly blended but do not overwork the dough. Cover and chill for 30 minutes.

$\mathscr{S}$weet Enriched Pie Pastry

—————————— PATE SUCREE ——————————

*T*his is a Pâte Brisée type of dough to which sugar is added. It is also called Pâte Sablée, which translates literally as "sandy paste." The amount of sugar can be varied in line with the sweetness of the filling. The higher the level of sugar that is used the more difficult the dough is to handle, but the crisper the baked pastry will be.

MAKES ¾ cup quantity

¾ cup all-purpose flour
small pinch of salt
5 tbsp unsalted butter, at room temperature
2 egg yolks, beaten
1–3 tbsp sugar

Make as for Pâte Brisée, adding the sugar with the egg yolks.

$\mathscr{E}$nriched Pie Pastry with Nuts

—————————— PATE FROLLEE ——————————

*A*lmonds are most frequently used in Pâte Frollée, but a similar pastry can be made using hazelnuts (filberts) or walnuts instead.

MAKES ¾ cup quantity

¾ cup all-purpose flour
small pinch of salt
4½ tbsp unsalted butter, at room temperature
1 egg yolk, beaten
½ cup freshly ground almonds
3 tbsp sugar (optional)

Make as for Pâte Brisée, adding the ground almonds and sugar with the egg yolk.

Choux Pastry

— PATE A CHOUX —

Choux pastry is quite unlike any other pastry – it is too soft to be rolled out so is piped or spooned to obtain the required shape and size.

MAKES 8 LARGE OR 16 SMALL BUNS

½ cup all-purpose flour
small pinch of salt
3 tbsp unsalted butter, diced
½ cup water
2–3 eggs, beaten

Sift the flour and salt together onto a sheet of wax paper. Gently heat the butter with the water until the butter has just melted, then bring quickly to a boil. Immediately draw the pan off the heat, add the flour in one go and beat vigorously with a wooden spoon or hand-held electric mixer until the flour is absorbed and the mixture forms a smooth, coherent mass. Stop beating immediately and return the pan to a very low heat for 30–60 seconds until the dough pulls cleanly away from the bottom and sides of the pan.

Remove the pan from the heat and allow the mixture to cool. Beat the mixture occasionally to hasten the cooling and to prevent a skin forming.

Gradually add the eggs, beating well after each addition and not adding more egg until the mixture has bound together again. Make sure all the mixture is included – if any adheres to the sides or bottom of the pan, or in the angle between the two, scrape it off and incorporate it. Continue adding egg until the dough is smooth, shiny and just falls softly from the spoon. Return the pan to a very low heat for 30–60 seconds, beating constantly, then leave to cool for 2–3 minutes before using.

uff Pastry

———— PATE FEUILLETEE ————

A very early form of puff pastry probably existed in ancient Greece, and flaky pastry cakes were mentioned in the Middle Ages, but it did not enter the realms of popular pastries until the seventeenth century. Two claims are made for its invention then, one attributing the pastry to a painter, Claude Gelée, and the other to a pastry cook in the house of Condé, named Feuillet.

MAKES ½ lb (1⅔ cup quantity)

1⅔ cups all-purpose flour
pinch of salt
1 tsp lemon juice
2 sticks (8 oz) unsalted butter

Sift the flour and salt together, then add the lemon juice and sufficient water to bind into a soft, pliable dough that is not sticky. Knead it into a smooth ball, cover and chill for 30 minutes.

Place the butter between two sheets of wax paper or plastic wrap and beat it with a rolling pin until it becomes soft and malleable and is a square ½ inch thick.

On a lightly floured surface using a lightly floured rolling pin, roll out the dough to a square about ¼ inch thick around the edges, with a slightly thicker pad of dough in the center. Place the butter on this pad and fold the sides of the dough around it, overlapping the edges very slightly so they meet in the center. Gently press the block of dough with the rolling pin at ½ inch intervals across its surface until it has grown slightly, then roll it out to a large rectangle.

Fold the two ends of the rectangle so they meet in the center, then fold the whole piece in half so that it resembles a book. Rotate this to the normal reading position of a book with the folded side as the spine. Cover and chill for 30 minutes.

Repeat the rolling and folding five times, chilling the dough after each one, then roll the dough once more before covering and chilling for at least 2 hours before giving the final shaping.

Genoese Sponge Cake

— PATE A GENOISE —

*B*utter that has been clarified makes a particularly fine sponge. To clarify, melt unsalted butter and skim off the froth from the surface, then carefully pour off the clear butter from the milky sediment in the pan. Leave the clarified butter to cool before using. The following quantity is sufficient for an 8–9 inch cake.

3 eggs
6 tbsp sugar
¾ cup cake flour
pinch of salt
4 tbsp unsalted butter, preferably clarified

Beat the eggs together lightly in a large bowl, then gradually beat in the sugar. Continue beating until the mixture is thick and light and will support the weight of a trail when the beater is lifted.

Sift the flour and salt over the egg mixture in two or three batches, folding in each batch quickly and lightly using a large metal spoon. Add the butter with the last batch. When just evenly blended, pour the mixture into a prepared pan, tap the pan firmly on the work surface and bake immediately.

Whisked Sponge Cake

— BISCUIT —

This is made using the same ingredients, in the same proportions, as a Genoese sponge. The difference lies in the way the eggs are added. The yolks are beaten with about three-quarters of the sugar; the whites are beaten separately until they are stiff, then the remaining sugar is sprinkled over the surface and beaten in until the whites are glossy. The whites are folded very lightly into the yolk mixture alternately with the flour and butter, using a large metal spoon, until just evenly blended.

This method produces a lighter, drier sponge. It is therefore more absorbent and so is particularly suitable for recipes in which the cake is moistened with a liqueur or syrup, before being assembled. A Genoese sponge is more springy and moist.

Italian or Cooked Meringue

—————— MERINGUE ITALIENNE ——————

*W*e know that meringue was being made before 1653 because in "Le Pâtissier François," published in that year and attributed to La Varenne, there is a recipe for "biscuits de sucre en neige" which resembles very closely modern meringue cookies.

MAKES ABOUT 80 SMALL MERINGUES

1 cup sugar
⅔ cup water
4 egg whites

Gently heat the sugar and water in a heavy-bottomed saucepan, stirring with a wooden spoon until the sugar has dissolved. Bring to a boil and boil, without stirring, until the temperature reaches 250°F on a candy thermometer, the hard ball stage. From time to time, wash down the sugar crystals that form on the sides of the pan using a dampened pastry brush.

Meanwhile, beat the egg whites until they are stiff enough to hold peaks when the beater is lifted and the surface looks moist – take care not to overbeat until the whites have become dry. Gradually pour the very hot syrup onto the egg whites, beating continuously, and continue to beat until the meringue has cooled completely.

Index